THE DOG SOLDIER'S MANUAL

A Practical Guide to Character Formation and the Cultivation of the Human Spirit

A Millennium Book

2 0 0 0

Raven Walker

Writers Club Press

San Jose · New York · Lincoln · Shanghai

Published by Writers Club Press, an imprint of iUniverse.com, Inc.

For information address:
iUniverse.com, Inc.
620 North 48th Street
Suite 201
Lincoln, NE 68504-3467
www.iuniverse.com

URL: http://www.writersclub.com

Dedicated To

The four Cheyenne dog soldiers who went out to meet Custer and certain violent death at the Little Bighorn ford to deny him the crossing and victory.

The 760 young men of the 1st and 3rd Ranger Battalions, wiped out at Cestera, Italy, infiltrating and fighting ten miles into the teeth two German divisions massed for a surprise counterattack, grinding it to a halt before it started.

Contents

ONE OF THE KIND

His name is James, and he lives among you, the people. When I first met him, he was lean, tall, and black, with a wonderfully resonant voice that could speak swiftly like a cheetah, and big, strong eyes, always looking around even when he was telling you a good story.

An Army brat raised in Japan, just out after six years as a U.S. Ranger, James was doing his best to conform, taking classes for a one year Tour and Travel degree at the college where I was just learning how to teach, migrating as I had, uninvited, to live at the foot of Pikes Peak. The college folded in the night on both of us.

We stayed in touch. James always had important observations to make, and was a good one to give encouragement. When I fluked into a fund raising walkathon for multiple sclerosis, a stranger in a strange town, with all the inherited sponsors backing out, James worked and walked five miles of strip highway America Academy Boulevard, asking strangers and store clerks if they would allow us to set up our brochures in any window bay or counter top that looked promising. Right in the middle of Desert Storm.

James walked everywhere. I saw him many times, ranging long stretches of the irregular, broken concrete terrain along side Academy, backpack near always full and pulled tight, loping along untroubled while the hot and confused traffic whipped by. Whoever he was with, his happiest purpose was to find one of those things to do only a strong, intelligent man can do, making a sure contribution to the commonweal, and doing it right away. He ran interference through the bureaucracies for his less determined friends, or stayed on a car problem until mobility was restored to those helpless before the sharking mechanic predators. His strong eyes were pleasing to watch, sitting tall, watching you and roving everywhere to keep an eye on anything and everything that was happening around us.

When I last saw James, five years later, he had grown into a Kodiak Bear of a man. If possible, his voice was deeper and throatier. On a sudden whim, I'd dropped into an auto parts store, and there he was, his back pack loaded with a new battery, and a three mile hike ahead to fix his girl-friend's sister's car. No hurry. We talked and laughed a good twenty min-utes catching up and telling stories.

When James was a soldier, he was a Ranger, an elite warrior. When he became a civilian, the citizen, James became Dog Soldier. He defended and protected his people. He helped those unable to help themselves. He craved such opportunities. He defended freedom not only on the fields of combat, but on the highways, streets and biways of Front Range America.

*****

It is not the purpose of this book to teach combat or war. That is best left to the warrior societies themselves, past and modern. Rather the goal is to set the true human foundation for the warrior. The skills of combat and war will change in response to new conditions, capabilities, and weaponary. But such proficiencies are futile unless they are melded to the heart and soul of a war-rior. And that achievement is available to all men, not just those who choose to become soldiers. That possibility is what this book is about.

There is more to being a warrior than war. More to being a soldier than combat. The modern world is a high risk zone full of contests, conflicts, sociopaths, predators, incompetence, corruption, deceit, and more kinds of bad fortune than the past has ever known. Easy to crackup and end up flaming in the ditch. Or disappear down a hole never to reappear. There are more than enough land mines, booby traps, ambushes, and nasty beaches to hit, ready or not. Keeping things together in modern society is like fighting a running guerrilla war. The heart and soul of the warrior is needed by every man, to fend alone, or to defend kith and kin. The Dog Soldier's Manual defines this kind of man, and identifies the paths of dis-cipline that breed him. If you really want to be a man, this is the place to start. The people never have too many dog soldiers.

THE BREEDING

ORIGINAL AMERICAN CHARACTER

One can hope that the unraveling of original American character will be a never ending challenge. But that remains to be seen. The conditions which shape the original American are like most others in the pagents of human history, neither permanent nor universal. Perhaps someday historians will write about the original American in much the same way as they now write about the Cheyenne Indians, of a strong and remarkable people who appeared for a brief moment in the malstrom of human survival, but who walk the earth no more. The bloodlines may continue, but the original character is gone.

Traits

The classic Frontier American was simple, direct, and genuine. Contrived complexity, indirection, hypocrisy and dissimulation, were arts practiced by the refined European aristocracy. To the practical, objective driven frontiersman, they were a waste of time, a sign of untrustworthiness and a lack of sand.

The frontier selected inhabitants who were adaptive and open to new ideas and practices. Yet oddly, they could be conservative as well. The rugged terrain, the hard climate, the strange plant and animal life, and the isolation required new ways of thinking and doing, just to have a chance at survival. At the same time, because the margin of success hung in such close balance, you stayed with what worked until the new ways proved out or flopped.

Consequently, the frontiersmen shared a stoic common sense, and combined that with a knack for the ingenious solution. They became incurably independent minded because it was the workings of their own minds that kept them alive and surviving. Yet they were tolerant. Others had a right to think and do as they chose. After all, it was their consequences to reap and deal with.

The result was a strong sense of self reliance. The Frontier American saddled their own broncs, fought their own fights, and generally survived and made it through the operations of their own minds and the competence of their own physical abilities. They were dogged and intrepid as needed. And adventuresome and highly mobile. To travel 20 miles to check out new territory was just another thing that needed to be done.

The frontier pioneer was industrious and productive, working hard just to make things work at all, and working to make things work better whenever possible. But this industry was not driven by guilt ridden penance, self-imposed in order to atone for Adam's Curse, original sin. Rather, one worked hard to increase the quality and comfort of living in rugged conditions, making life more ample and enjoyable. One worked hard to have free time to enjoy as they wished. This was their own time, time they had earned for themselves to enjoy the sufficiencies their labors had produced. This was to drink and feast upon liberty. What good would freedom be if one still lived and acted like the serfs and drudges still bound to the land in Europe, their time not their own, but their masters'.

Frontier folk were children of freedom, freedom of the most forbidding type, thrown out upon the rugged land with only their own resources and inventiveness to sink or swim. What the survivors created was a culture of freedom and free enterprise, one free speaking and intensely libertarian, with all sharing a basic equality, where all had a right to prove themselves and where none had a right to look upon themselves as inherently better or superior to any other man. Your business was yours and none of their's, and vice versa.

All this confluence of frontier conditions and the adaptive pioneer response had a remarkable, creative effect on the language. The American speaks metaphorically, using dozens of figures of speech drawn from the breaking realities of life occurring all around. Any analogy that is apt and aptly stated becomes a part of the common lingo, soon known and used by all. Further, the American cuts down so much the number of syllables and words employed that the easy drawl found throughout all regions of the country becomes possible. Hence the wry, dead pan style of humor. America invented the humorist. On the far frontier, without newspapers, radio or television, one learns entertainment from one's sense of humor and its skillful expression, to the pleasure of others and one's self.

Finally, the Original American must be counted among the Hard to Kill types. Though the Indians did their best to terrorize and decimate frontier settlements, murdering hundreds upon hundreds of men, women and children from ambush and surprise attack, more came to try themselves, and those that survived not only held their ground, they up and moved West as soon as they were able.

THE BREEDING GROUNDS

You just cannot be born and grow up to be an original American. Rather, the American Character is a progressive response, over time, to demanding conditions, conditions of stark freedom, challenge and adversity. There are no racial preferences or prerequisites. Background matters little. Wherever you find these conditions confronting good human stock, you will find the metamorphosis and the emergent American character.

The American Frontier

By European standards of the day, the American Frontier was an untamed land, full of strangeness, danger and the great unknown. It could swallow up whole families. Living conditions were hostile and raw. The pioneer walked out onto the frontier with nothing but what they carried with them, no shelter, no secure food supply, and plenty of adversity to cope with before having even the slightest chance of surviving. You were free and independent ready or not. Add to this the enmity of the Indian, upon whose traditional lands you encroached, as bent to defend and preserve their way of life as the pioneer was in making a go of it.

A narrow application of the ways and culture of Old Europe simply wouldn't cut it. Significant adaptation was necessary in order to first survive, and then to succeed. The pioneer made these adaptations on their own. Consequently, they proved to be independent, self reliant, hardy spirits, observant and open to new possibilities in the practical attainment of practical objectives.

Any frontier breeds strong, freedom loving people, comprised of hard to kill, original individuals, ready to fight to keep what they have won.

Modern Proving Trails

The geographic American Frontier was officially closed in 1890. Already long gone were the geographical basis of the tribe and its enemies. One can and must still have lines of Kinship throughout society, but they are now geographically interspersed among all regions and realms of society. Likewise, the face of the enemy can no longer be easily identified. Interspersion is simply one of the playing conditions of modern society.

But wherever frontier conditions occur, conditions of hard earned freedom, challenge and adversity, there you find original Americans in the making. Great events like the building of the Alaskan pipeline drew tens of thousands of strangers together in rugged, wide open, demanding circumstances. On a smaller scale, Americans remain mobile, and will up and move to new cities and regions, invited or not. Each little interior migration carries a piece of the old frontier with it. The same is true for the struggles of new immigrants coming into the country from abroad, for blacks breaking free from the ghetto, and for women brushing up against the glass ceiling. And we all know that the streets of the inner city hold a terrible and demanding set of playing conditions, as hard and as dangerous as any provided by the old frontier.

In a softer way, all the game fields of America are frontier turf, the baseball diamonds, the chess boards, the football fields, basketball courts and the classrooms. Ultimately, in modern society, the frontier is individual and appears wherever any free person sets for themselves a quest, an adventure, or a great achievement, instead of accepting expected roles, conforming uncritically to what others say you should say, think, and do.

THE CHEYENNE

Shakespeare wrote great tragedies, Hamlet, Othello, MacBeth, where once greatness of spirit is brought down by the irrevocable operation of fate, history and human nature. But it falls to actual human history to write the greatest epics and the greatest tragedies of all. Such were the Cheyenne. To themselves, they were the Tsistsistas, the people.

From the beginning, the Cheyenne were a westering, vanguard people, never large in number, poor and martially weak, but holding together to the bitter end. Speaking a brand of the Algonquin language family, they were the most widely dispersed of the Algonquin languages, which radiate from a center some where in Quebec. No one knows for sure their early whereabouts. One map places them on the Illinois prairie during the 1500's. Later, this territory will be fiercely held and defended by the Miami and the Shawnee before they are rubbed out by the Long Knives.

By the 1700's, the Cheyenne are in the north, in the upper Great Lakes region, fishing mostly, miserable and very poor. From there begins the great migration of cultural memory. They pull up stakes and head West again, encountering a great marshy spread of endless water. But scouts find and mark a way across the barrier, and the people crossed, emerging in the northern woodlands of Minnesota, near the boundary to the Great Plains, the ancestral homelands of the Souix. Here they adopt a semi-agricultural life, making their first excursions onto the plains to hunt buffalo. Life was stable and good, the people well fed and no longer poor. But the press of the white people is now felt. Tribes from the north, from Canada, attack, raid, and push the Cheyenne, just as they were being pushed by the whites. Only they have guns, and the Cheyenne have no chance standing against them. Having caught up with the Souix by moving westward, the Cheyenne now pass them and venture out onto the plains for good, where they will undergo an extraordinary metamorphosis.

Thrusting deep into a new, strange environment, alien to the river, lake, and woodlands environs of their past, the Cheyenne not only adapted and survived, they flourished and grew stronger, taking to the big game, nomadic lifestyle as if born to it. Soon they acquire and master the horse. So commanding they become that they drive the Crow and Kiowa before them until they have conquered the Blacks Hills for their homeland.

Through facing and meeting the challenges, adversities, and the unknown, leaving their past behind, their future to be found in what lie ahead, the Cheyenne became a strong and vigorous people. In their new world, they were free, well provided, and free to range its spacious, beautiful lands. Such life, liberty and hard earned happiness creates a powerful motivation to protect, defend, and keep that freedom. The ferocity of the Cheyenne warrior in attack and defense became an envied legend to all their enemies, white and Indian. None were more feared.

But the Cheyenne remained a small people, and in time, the larger, more populous Souix followed them out onto the plains, pushing the Cheyenne off to the buffalo ranges between the Platte and the Arkansas. Yet as diplomatically wise as they were fierce, the Cheyenne made lasting peace with both the Souix to the north and the Kiowa to the south, even though both these surrounding nations spoke entirely different languages.

This final move placed the Cheyenne right square in the middle of the coming steamroller of westward white migration.

Ways

At the time the Cheyenne society became defined and unified, a cultural hero appears, Sweet Medicine, who like a Moses or a Solon, lays down the principal cultural practices and organization of Cheyenne society. Each of the ten bands are governed by four chiefs, with four, higher chiefs governing the tribe as a whole. This system fit the nomadic, big game hunter-gatherer life well. As the bands separated, each possessed their own autonomous leadership, yet each were still a part of the larger tribal identity and its governance.

Leadership was a consensual process, amongst the chiefs themselves, and between the chiefs and the people. The chiefs ruled by wisdom, not authority. The real chiefs were those who had followers. If some of the people chose to set up their lodges next to yours, you led. It was boasted among the Cheyenne that no chief could tell any Cheyenne what to do. The first rule of Cheyenne society was that of kinship.

While the biological family, as always, makes the first unit of social organization, the loyalty and caring of the natural family was the standard and rule for all of the people. The Cheyenne were one people, all one kin, all caring, considering, and supporting each other without compunction. There were no real poor, for it was the duty of kinship to see that even the weakest, the helpless, and the unfortunate were properly supplied in the basic wants. Each made their contribution to the people and were respected and valued.

To fail in kinship virtues was to court shame and disapprobation. To kill another Cheyenne, or be responsible for the same, meant automatic banishment from the tribe and all bands forever. In this sense, the Cheyenne practiced the eugenics of true brotherhood. Any Cain was removed from the gene pool.

On the other side of eugenics, the Cheyenne were an open society biologically. Captives and strays from other tribes, races or peoples were readily adopted into Cheyenne society and accorded kinship. To live Cheyenne was to be Cheyenne. At the time of their destruction, the Cheyenne were of as mixed blood as an average American today.

Among Cheyenne men, four virtues were revered and practiced, bravery, fortitude, generosity and wisdom. These were the standards by which the individual would be judged. Among the women were added honesty and fertility.

Home life was based on female blood lines. When a couple were married, they moved in with her family, perhaps in the same lodge, perhaps in their own just next door. The home, the lodge, belonged to the woman, and if she became seriously dissatisfied with her husband, she had only to throw out his possessions to divorce him. Perhaps this feminine domination of domestic life balanced the studied aggression needed in the male.

While the Cheyenne, or any Plains Indian, were not demonstrative people, affection was genuine. A wife beater would surely get promptly divorced and suffer much shame, perhaps living in the bushes for many nights before venturing up the courage to show himself. Neither were children physically punished. It was thought unnecessary and a sign that the offending parent was incapable of using successfully the methods of shame, persuasion, wisdom, reason, and positive encouragement. Since there have been few peoples as strong and brave as the Cheyenne, sparing the rod obviously does not spoil the child if the parenting process is intelligent fulfilled. To the Cheyenne, the European's ferocious corporal punishment was a tacit admission of parenting failure.

Quality of Life

In the high noon of Cheyenne destiny, life was good. With the abundance of the buffalo and the resourcefulness of the people in finding and making all else they needed, the Cheyenne enjoyed a material surplus and comfort that was at the same time simple and uncomplicated, easy to break down and move as the seasons required. To have too many possessions, save horses, was considered a failure of character.

eously on any notable occasion, and celebrated their achievements and victories over their enemies with relish and enthusiasm. The Cheyenne experienced well balanced emotional satisfaction and spiritual peace. They lived hard and died hard, and honored the entire process.

Such a transformation in a people does not take place without their awareness of what is happening. The Cheyenne had a clear and strong sense of their greatness and goodness. In the discerning eyes of others, they were called the beautiful people, not just for their looks, but for their ways and manners as well. They were considered to have the most virtuous women and the wisest and most thoughtful leaders, their word good far beyond the word of any white man of their day. The Cheyenne were said to be of noble character, possessing the fiercest warriors, the hardest charging horsemen, and they proved, in the end, the hardest to kill. More than any other tribe, they had to be exterminated in total so defiant and determined were they in keeping the life that had made them great.

The Warrior Societies

Like all Plains Indians, the Cheyenne possessed the warrior societies that were an integral part of male culture in tribal life. These societies soaked up rouge males, and showcased the culture of martial leadership and fellowship. Among the Cheyenne, there were originally four, created and defined by Sweet Medicine, the Bow Strings, the Fox Soldiers, the Red Shields, and the Elk Soldiers.

Each society kept its own lodge and sacred possessions. Each had its own distinct rituals, ceremonies, and regalia. Each recognized and honored the deeds and valor of its members with badges and emblems of distinction for public view and honor. During great communal events, like moving to new campsites, the communal buffalo hunts, or on tribal war campaigns, the warrior societies would be assigned police duties by the chiefs. One to lead, two to flank, and one to watch the rear. During these times, a mild form of martial law existed. Discipline was required to keep the tribe functioning as a whole, so the societies were granted the right to physically coerce, through threat or quirt, members of the tribe deviating from the prescribed plan. For serious violations, the lodge of the offending culprit could be destroyed, though through generosity, the offenders were usually restored to domestic competence.

But the soldier bands rarely fought together. War parties were mixed, and actual war, a free form affair. The warrior societies did not become a tactical grouping until through a tragic act worthy of a Greek tragedy, the Dogmen were changed from a warrior society into a functioning village band of their own.

THE DOG SOLDIERS

To themselves, they were the Dogmen. To the American soldiers, they were the Dog Soldiers, the natural warrior's recognition and admiration of martial prowess and equality. Their origins are independent from the other four warrior societies. The Dogmen were established sometime after the culture hero's time by an unknown warrior, who returned from a vision quest with the vision of a new warrior society, setting down its rules, rituals, and regalia. Black Crow Feathers became the token emblem of membership. By the time of the white man, the Dogmen societies were to be found throughout nearly all the Plains tribes. The Dogmen were a pan tribal phenomena, appearing wherever men chose to follow their ways. A splinter group, the Crazy Dogs, were known as the toughest and the wildest of all, perhaps like the tradition of the bizerker in Viking warrior lore.

The Dogmen specialized in rearguard action, protecting the fleeing or moving people. Often they used the Dog Rope, tied to their neck and staked to ground in the path of the oncoming enemy, the vow, to fight to the death for as long as possible.

A remarkable cultural transformation occurred in 1837. Porcupine Bear, the chief of the Dogmen, broke up a quarrel and blood fight between two young dogmen by killing the weaker one. No Cheyenne is allowed to kill another Cheyenne, with no exceptions, not even by accident, without suffering permanent banishment from the band and the tribe. The offenders would thereafter have to camp alone, a slow but sure death sentence in lands of sudden harshness and enemy war parties.

But as a true chief with a real following, when Porcupine Bear moved his lodge away, all the dogmen moved their lodges with him. Shortly after, in a whole tribe attack on the Kiowa and Comanche, in a separate, somewhat distant engagement, the Dogmen won a dramatic victory more decisive than that accomplished by the tribal engagement. Many more new lodges showed up at the Dogmen's camp. The warrior society became a band, a self governing, self sustaining village in their own right. But a new rule of band affiliation was put into effect, males joined the Dogmen Band and brought their wives with them.

The Dogmen Band remained at total war with the encroaching masses of amalgamated European descendants, the most blood thirsty, ferocious, uncompromising, defiant and wildest of all Cheyenne. When the Cheyenne divided into the Northern and Southern branches for good, the Northern joining the Souix far above the Platte, and Southern joining the Kiowa far below the Arkansas, the Dogmen Band remained on the central range, dead center between the Platte and the Arkansas.

Through the irony of history, the Dogmen Band played out the mission of their warrior society on a grand scale. They doggedly held out on their range when all kin had fled nearly a thousand miles away in opposite directions, holding their ground right in the center of the surging path of the Western migration, as if tied on a dog rope, until finally in deliberate carelessness born of inevitable fate, the Dogmen village allowed itself to be surprised one morning in 1875 by the Bluecoat Calvary, and was summarily demolished. Some survivors went North, and some went South. The people were permanently split asunder, and defeated in detail.

THE AMERICAN RANGER

The same spontaneous expression of male culture that occurred among the Cheyenne and their Dogmen, occurred among the American pioneer. These warriors, too, came from out of the people, ready and capable of war and extraordinary valor in defense of the freedom and safety of the people. They were called Rangers.

Though the Rangers appeared as an identifiable fighting force as early as 1675 in the "King Phillip's War", their defining origins occur in 1756 under Major Robert Rogers during the French and Indian War. Rogers personally recruited his men from the original American frontiersmen of his day, and through his 28 rules of common sense and his 19 standing orders on readiness, security, and tactics, he created the basis for Ranger culture and conduct still followed today. He was like the unknown Cheyenne who established the Dogmen.

Under Rogers, the Rangers became known for their solid preparation and bold movement. He even conducted a training program in the application of his rules that included live fire exercises. When other troops went into winter quarters, Roger's Rangers found the enemy and attacked.

Morgan's Rangers

The lesson of the inherent fighting ability to be found in the rugged frontiersman was not lost on Washington. One of his first initiatives upon taking command of the fledgling Contintental Army was to ask Daniel Morgan, a reputed Virginia frontiersman, to recruit several companies of men like himself from the colonial frontier. Their primary role was to act as Washington's eyes and ears, to range great distances, infiltrate, raid, and carry out reconnaissance. They supplied their own rifle, knife, clothes and personal gear, and were expected to be able to feed themselves off the land if necessary.

The British complained bitterly about the American guerrilla warfare tactics. It was uncivilized and low down. But their complaint was against the Rangers who conducted this warfare, not the Continental European style troops. Only the Rangers could be reliably counted upon to carry the war to the enemy, reminding them how much at mortal risk they were.

But the impact of the Rangers was far more significant than mere scouting. They were the hidden decisive advantage of the Revolutionary War, though never fully utilized because not enough men qualified. At Frayser's Farm at the Battle of Saratoga, in the forests of upper New York, the Rangers decimated the attacking British lines from distant cover, out of reach and unstoppable. When Benedict Arnold rallied the final charge, he was just cleaning up the demoralizing destruction already delivered by the Rangers. If Washington had had 10,000 Rangers Mammoth Courthouse during the British slow retreat through New Jersey, from Philadelphia back to New York, Lexington and Concord would have been repeated on a grand scale, and the War won that summer.

Clark's Rangers

Another Revolutionary War Ranger Force was recruited under George Rogers Clark, an accomplished Kentucky frontiersmen, under the auspices of Patrick Henry, the Governor of Virginia at the time. This force was drawn from the trans-appalachian settlements, and scarcely numbered more than a hundred during most of its actions.

Through stealth and secrecy, Clark's Rangers journeyed a thousand miles to surprise and capture the villages of Kaskaskia and Vincennes along the Mississippi in southern Illinois. When the British descended from Detroit to recapture Vincennes, the Rangers made a 100 mile march in mid winter, through wildly flooded swamps and river bottoms to surprise and cage the British force, picking it to death slowly through marksmanship, completely out of range of the smooth bore muskets of the redcoats. The British surrender gave the entire Northwest territories to the new nation.

The Revolutionary War Ranger was experienced in frontier survival, an expert marksmen, self provident, highly mobile, capable of handling the shock of hand to hand combat, but too wily to be drawn into such. With the rifle, one could stand off from the enemy, fire from cover, and riddle their ranks without risking the force. These Rangers came from out of the people, the American pioneers, the dog soldiers of the kinship, warriors ready made by the frontier and its demanding conditions of survival. Like the dog soldier, their home was with the people, and the freedom of the people, their freedom as well.

At King's Mountain, in Western South Carolina, an apparently unorganized force of over the mountain men decimated a British and Tory column, much like the Souix and Cheyenne overwhelmed Custer. The important observation to make concerning the early American Ranger is that they were an elite fighting force that came that way, whether they organized themselves as a corp, or simply banded together as individuals.

The Texas Rangers

The next appearance of Rangers as a significant military force occurred with the formation of the Texas Rangers in 1836 by the new Republic of Texas. Their mission was to protect the frontier from depredations by Mexican patriots and the Comanche Indians.

These Rangers, too, were recruited from out of frontier society, this time, experienced plainsmen and mounted. Like their Revolutionary War predecessors, they supplied their own rife, knife, pistol, camp gear, and horse. The favored method of operation was to track and trail without tiring, to ride hard, achieve surprise, and to go in on the attack, full speed, firing Walker Colt revolvers at point blank range for total shock. They seldom needed to employ long range mobile rifle fire they were capable of delivering.

During the Mexican War, the Texas Rangers were the eyes and ears, and the terrible raiders, for both Zachery Taylor's army in Northern Mexico and Winfield Scott's at Mexico City. At the Battle of Buena Vista with Taylor, the encircling movement by the Ranger force, attacking the rear echelons of the Mexican Army was the decisive turning movement. The Mexicans feared and dreaded the Rangers more than they feared the Apache. At least the Apache occasionally took prisoners for slaves.

The Confederate Rangers

Perhaps it is one of history's fitting ironies that the next and last significant Ranger force for the next 80 years would fight for the South in their failed War of Independence. In truth, the South advanced the culture of Ranger warfare in both directions, to larger corps and astonishingly effective raiding units.

While the mounted forces under Nathan Bedford Forrest were never named Rangers—he usually commanded 10,000 troops or more—the character of his operations and tactics, and their stunning impact was all Ranger. His famous dictum, "Get there fustest with the mostest", still defines the essence of tactical combat, no matter the scale of operations. Patton said much the same thing, but had to use a lot more words.

At the other end, the Rangers under Moseby, the Grey Ghosts, operated in the traditional Ranger manner, raids, reconnaissance, deep infiltrations, and constant disruptions. Moseby could keep ten times his number of the enemy occupied, and once attacked and routed an entire Union regiment in bivouac, over 500 men, with only nine of his own.

Darby's Rangers

In World War II, the idea of the warrior ranger was resurrected after a long period of neglect. This time the men were recruited in the terms of modern society. Volunteers from the regular ranks were sought, individuals willing to commit themselves to the rigors and discipline necessary to produce an elite fighting force. They were trained as commandos in Scotland, particularly in amphibious operations. Colonel Darby, their organizer, however, added two classic American Ranger rules, self reliance and common sense. The Ranger was to do what needed to be without being told, and to do the sane thing in the absence of higher authority.

During the invasion of Sicily, the Darby's Rangers fulfilled their mission of advance infiltration and suddenly concentrated firepower in achieving key landing zone objectives. But their higher mettle was soon tested, for they were the only force available to fight off a concerted counterattack by the Herman Goering Panzer Division while the main invasion force was still fumbling its way out of the beachhead.

At the Salerno invasion in Italy, the Rangers secured the mountainous Sorrento Peninsula, just their element, on the north flank of the beachhead, and bottled up and confounded ten times their number of the enemy.

But at Anzio, they met with a disaster unrivaled in military history. They were nearly massacred to the man, advancing forward. Not even Picket's Charge at Gettysburg matches this ordeal, for the Rangers had to fight for every mile they advanced. Their mission had been to infiltrate and raid in advance of a full scale breakout offensive, ten miles to the village of Cisterna. But they ran head on into a massing, full scale German counterattack, completely unsuspected by military intelligence, a couple of heavy divisions against a couple of battalions. But they kept on attacking forward, dodging the enemy forces, then striking hard and moving on, long after the main attack had stalled jumping off. A few reached the objective, the outskirts of Cesterna, before the inevitable odds finally caught up with them. Six walked back out alive out of 760 who went in.

The two day battle, against odds that should have precluded any battle at all, forced the enemy to commit all their reserves as if meeting a major offensive in massive numbers, and stalled the counterattack for two more days. These Rangers were like the Cheyenne teenagers on the last day of Cheyenne Autumn, their story soon to be told. They were indomitable, without fear, and very hard to kill. Is it any wonder why the motto, "Live free or die", is so understandable. But only those who have lived a free life can see it and know its power.

THE AMERICAN PIONEER

The people from out of whom the Ranger arose were the American Pioneers. Like the Cheyenne, they boldly set out into unknown lands, forbidding and challenging. Like the Cheyenne, the frontier conditions made those who survived strong, self reliant, and independent, an entirely new kind of human being, at least from the narrow European point of view.

Like the Cheyenne, the American pioneer was a westerly, vanguard people, on the move to escape the petty oppressions of European culture and its moments of repressive tyranny. A people who, once discovering the boons of freedom no matter the hardships endured, became impossible to subjugate again without extreme physical prejudice. The very act of survival and success laid the foundations and character of real warriors, ready made to defend the people and their way of life. True freedom isn't just worth fighting for. If you know and experience it, there is no other choice.

Daniel Boone

The American pioneer, while resembling the Cheyenne in character, introduced the first elements of the modern social condition, that of interspersion. They were not a concentrated tribe, but were dispersed, banding together at times, yet separating again as the seasons passed. Consequently, the cultural icons of the American frontier were far more intensely individualistic than were the seaboard Founding Fathers. Daniel Boone is an excellent example. Boone is the archetype of the Western American and the prototype of the indigenous dog soldier.

Born and bred to the frontier, its freedoms and wonders, Boone committed himself to blazing the trails and building the first secure settlement, Boonesborough, west of the Appalachians, making those same freedoms and wonders available to any and all who would dare start life anew on the forbidding frontier. These people were his kinship. The lawyers came later.

Daniel Boone himself would be dubious at this elevation of his life to that of cultural hero. He saw himself as a thoroughly common man, no different from many other extremely capable men on the frontier of his day. It was largely a matter of happenstance that during one hunting season, a struggling writer joined Boone's camp, desparate to find some sensational story that would earn his way fare to New York City. Apparently Boone was in a talking mood, the tales were published, and the popular legend of Daniel Boone was born. The civilized East now had a name upon which to hang all that wild Western frontiersmen stuff, and a name to use when making up more of the fabulous bunk. Boone insisted to the end that everything that came after the first publication was a "bunch of damned lies". The legend itself never did Boone any good. It only made him a clear target for the lawyers.

But the conditions that made Boone's life are the classic molding forces that shape dog soldiers, rangers, and pioneers. As a boy, out in the woods of Massachusetts and Pennsylvania, Boone was often left alone on the outpost farm for weeks at a time, only cows and the forest for company. As is natural to the curious human novitiate, Boone spent days away on his own and became one with the land. Where he could hunt, he could live. As a teenager, Boone was along on the disastrous Braddock campaign during the French and Indian War. Like most of the milita that sensibly fled the massacre, Boone made the 300 mile trek back through the Pennsylvania wilderness in good shape.

After the Revolutionary War, Boone's people moved down to the Blue Ridge Mountains of the Western Carolinas. It was here that Boone's legendary trail blazing began. He crossed often through the Cumberland Gap into the rich hunting grounds of Kentucky and Tennesee and never got lost. He gained the reputation there of being the best hunter in the

Blue Ridge region. Even in his seventies, on the Missouri frontier, when hunting with younger men, Boone's take was always among the best because he knew how to find the deer.

Boone lived an active life well into grand old age. At eighty, an observer found him hard at work by the fireplace, carving out a new powder horn. "Got to get ready for the fall hunt", Boone explained. Thanks largely to his fame, lawyers were able to take every acre of the tens of thousands he had laid claim to in Kentucky. He was not even left a reservation. Essentially homeless, Boone spent his last years, walking from one relative's house to another, spending a week here, or two weeks there, on the same legs strong from long use roaming hundreds of thousands of miles through the wildernesses of the early American frontier. Somedays, he would just disappear for a week between visits. Even in his eighties, where Boone could hunt, he could live, and be happy in the provident solitude. Not even the lawyers could finish him off. Hard to kill.

Modern Kinship

While the American pioneer did bond occasionally along geographical lines, with neighbors taking on the vestments of kinship as truly as any tribal citizen, they arrived on the frontier as individuals. Consequently, the social belonging process was somewhat free form. Some neighbors were not good neighbors at all. There was no automatic extension of the rule of kinship. Not all of the population surrounding one are one's people. Some of them may actually be hazardous to any kinship. But people will bond. They will have kinships.

The biological family remains the inner circle of kinship, but over time, even this is dispersed in modern society. So we seek and find others whom we can trust enough to treat in the kinship way, wherever we can, with strengthening bonds of kinship developing from the outer circles of strangers and acquaintances to the inner circles of friends and brothers.

We try many, and find a few. Some persons never catch on to the virtues and benefits of the genuine exchange processes of kinship living.

We may meet true kindred spirits, sometimes for only a brief time in our lives, but any kinship known and experienced never dies. Others we would be close to are out there, even if we never run into them. What counts is that if we did, the kindred sense would know. The modern condition of interspersion is only slightly inconvienent.

THE EUROPEAN SOCIAL DISEASE

On the leveling frontier, mem stand side by side. In contrast, in the urban centers, men stand upon each other's back, climbing the ladder of social distinctions like frantic monkeys scrambling to make the top of the tree before it topples over. Imposed upon society is the order of hierarchical classes, ultimately castes, each superior in kind from the ranks below. In the Old World, the lowest clas often contains those people who were first conquered long ago when the mad scrambles first started. This approach to social organization is caused bywhat might be aptly called the European Social Disease.

In any instance or case whatsoever, where any person, or people, set themselves above and beyond another person, or people, on the presumption that they are better, inherently superior, more righteous and wise, even God's chosen ones, in any form or subtle manifestation, under any contrived rationale, simply to justify an unjust action, an unfair policy, or a prejudicial attitude toward these presumed lesser beings, the European Social Disease has caught hold. Under any name you might prefer, the betrayal of our common humanity is the same. Indeed, this affliction of spirit and character threatens to destroy the original individual and real human freedom wherever these might be found. If it proves a terminal disease, one the human species cannot rise above, the Great American Experiment will die slowly, like a once mighty oak now banished to the desert, until it finally becomes a mere historical conjecture.

The European Social Disease cultivates and embraces a culture of conformity, the true antithesis of a culture of freedom. The conformity is contrived and employed to command, domineer, and subjugate other humans, to make sure that they remain the inferior they are cast to be. A permanent ruling class is then both necessary and a responsibility of the elite. We will be controlled for our own good.

This Disease presumes a permanent hierarchy among humanity. That the first should, and will always, be first, and that the last, always and necessarily, the last. Some men shall be masters, and the rest, their servants and slaves. Such is the natural order of things. Upon each head is placed the foot of another, more highly placed, and so on from top to bottom throughout society.

This disease of character is the basis of all social injustice, oppression, class privilege, inhumanity and unequal rights. This is the society of a permanent, insulated ruling class, lording it over the masses, the common people. To the pretenders, humanity is simply a great hive of drones to be controlled to their pleasure and forced into the artificial conformity of their lies. This is what the American Pioneer fled West to escape, what the American Revolution was supposedly going to do away with.

Much work and energy is spent by those suffering this disease in identifying and grading the many necessary ranks of hierarchical society. One must have clear standards of conformity to signify status. Besides the hording of wealth and power, clothes, etiquette, even manner of speech, are employed to discern the noble and worthy from the uncouth and unwashed.

In fairness to the Europeans, they did not invent this malediction, this blight upon the human soul. Virtually all "civilizations" which are built up by conquest and exploitation, suffer this disease. But between European Imperialism and the arrogance of their missionaries, they infected the world with the evil of self righteousness, presumed superiority, and therefore, the right to rule and subjugate. No European of those days would dare say no chief could tell them what to think and do. Such defiance meant death, often an ugly one.

The Spanish monks of the New World quite literally indentured the native Indians to the farm fields surrounding their monasteries, making them virtual slaves. Those that ran away were run down and killed by the conquistadors. America itself, too much a European wannabe, was delighted and proud to have its own "little brown brothers" in the

Phillipines to take of for their own good. The persistence of slavery long after even the Europeans had given it up as morally wrong, and the obliteration of the American Indian Natives, seal our guilty, infected state. We were spawned out of Europe and still cannot escape its ugly crudities.

There is no biological or psychological basis to the belief that some given group or segment of humanity is inherently superior to most others. We are all cut from the same cloth, the homo sapian species, with all the same massive imperfections. We can be as cutely trainable as chimpanzees, and as stupid as cows.

Cultures and societies differ widely in their accumulation of wealth, material technologies, and the scale of governmental organizations. Some cultures are tribal, and some think they are "civilized", perhaps the greatest delusion of all. But in even the so called primitive cultures, one often finds real wisdom in the business of being human, in handling discordant social relations, and in the attainment of moral virtue. When one considers the unbelievable, compulsive insanity of the European in WWI, where after four years and the violent deaths of ten million young males, their generals still had no idea that direct assaults on well entrenched machine gun nests did not work, one could easily argue that the European system is one of the poorest examples of human society so far occurring, despite the grand art their pirate's treasure could afford. When George Washington said, "Beware of European entanglements", what he meant was that these people were sick and crazy, and any association with them would surely lead to any number of unnatural disasters their insanity was bound to create, dragging America unnecessarily down with them. Why endure an arduous and painful War of Independence just to sign up for more stupidity of the same?

Unfortunately, despite the theoretically wonderful American political revolution, much of the country is deeply infected by the European Social Disease. The insidious Social Darwinism flourished here, even after England, its original home, rejected it. The Robber Barons and their ilk of the post Civil War Industrial Revolution loved it. Social Darwinsim told them that they were inherently superior beings because they had acquired great wealth, and promised them salvation because of the same, for God rewarded his chosen few by material riches on this earth. And of the labor drones who created this wealth out of their time and toil? That was their necessary fate. To try to raise them above that was futile for their natural inferiority would prevent them for knowing and keeping what bounties were granted them. Why else do we have inferiors, except for the many to elevate the few.

The much noted, often bragged about, Puritan streak is another ugly example. After resisting and fighting for their religious freedom against the punitive suppressions of the Anglican British, the Puritans withdrew to Massachusetts, gladly and freely punishing any deviants from their perfect creed and its prescribed patterns of conformity with a vengeance only God is supposed to exercise. When God said, "Only ye without sin cast the first stone", the Puritans all threw at once. On a per capita basis, the pious and righteous of Salem burned more heretics, witches and humbugs than the Spanish Inquisition managed. When you can willingly, and with pious intent, hurt, harm or disparage others for holding and speaking differing ideas and beliefs from yours, for looking and acting in ways strange to yours, believing all the while you are righteously doing God's work for him, this is the European Social Disease in full bloom.

There are enormous inequalities in human nature, but they are largely just differences. What they are is individual. We are all first formed from the same basic human animal. Everything after that is just detail. This fundamental equality in human experience and worth does not preclude judgments as to better at this or worse at that. One has to see the truth of things. The key is to understand that such judgments are individual. We each may be judged, and will be, by how we perform, act and conduct ourselves, toward ourselves and others. But no undue privilege or favor should be expected. Not in a just, free society.

The Soldier Drone

A culture of conformity, with all its subtle coercions, its lies, sub-terfuges, and ultimate brute force, is hard, very hard, on the human spirit. Through the Big Lie and its vigorous selling, the ruling class compro-mises, then breaks, then finally destroys, the human spirit. The queens must have a hive of well trained drones.

But the oppressions found in cultures of conformity have also proved the essential nature of the human spirit, that it is born free and only lives best when free. Despite extraordinary efforts at repression, individuals rise up in opposition, usually martyred directly, then groups band together and are massacred. Then finally, the common people, as nearly one, as dumb as they can ever be, as malleable and compliant as they might seem, rebel, even revolt, and either win freedom or are exterminated. The only truly satisfying condition of humankind is that of freedom which implies an essential equality within the species. All else is incidental and will prove so in the end.

The European Social Disease does not lend itself to breeding warriors, at least not reliably. One of the great and decisive turning points of the American Revolutionary War occurred after Washington was ignomin-iously forced to retreat across the whole of New Jersey, with desertions, lost stragglers, and expired enlistments shrinking his army to the point where he had only dog soldiers left. But Washington apparently knew the quality of what he had, for he sicced his dog soldiers on the unsuspecting Hessians, the well drilled drones hired by King George III to spare a little British blood. The contest was no contest, and the victory at Trenton revived a cause that surely looked lost for good.

This is no knock on the great traditions of the common soldier to be found throughout European history. Sound human male stock will learn to fight and will do so tenaciously. The instinct for self preservation assures this. But there are no dog soldier or ranger traditions in Imperialist

European "Civilization". The soldier did not spontaneously arise out of the culture of the people. He had to be conscripted and trained like a mule.

The far more serious shortcomings stemming from the disease are to be found in the command leadership. Here the disease manifests itself in profound arrogance. The enemy, because they are by nature, inferior, are presumed to be incurably weak hearted, cowardly, and easily frightened and overawed by the superior culture's mere presence, thus violating the first rule of military strategy. Never underestimate the will and ability of the enemy. You must assume they are as smart and as brave as you. Most military debacles, Viet Nam included, begin by ignoring this rule.

The history of British military arrogance during the Imperial Era, and its persistence despite dramatic lessons to the contrary, is notable, beginning with Braddock's massacre in the wilds of Pennsylvania by merely a quarter of his own forces, to disasters in Afghanistan, the Orange Free State, against the Ashanti on the Gold Coast of Africa, against the Zulu and the Turks, and against the self freed slaves of Haiti. Even though the soon to be conquered people must give in the mass production technology and the sheer number of excess males that an imperial culture can squander, people truly free show up with real warriors and bury the drones in far greater numbers that they themselves finally suffer. When the drones of ruling class take the field and its command, ripe with the disease, no intelligent military strategy is possible. While the European Social Disease is personally satisfying if you are to the manner born, it is decidedly dysfunctional when dealing with the real world outside the urban hive. Invariably, it leads to class warfare, rebellion, ugly reaction, and disaster.

CHEYENNE AUTUMN

The end for the Cheyenne came like a ten ton steel door slamming shut, like a hurricane relentlessly pounding the shore until the last grain of sand is stripped away.

The Martyrdom of Black Kettle

Black Kettle was an elder chief, one of the Big Bellies, and the leader of the Southern Cheyenne. Known as a kind, thoughtful, and generous wise man, Black Kettle was an early and persistent advocate for peace with the whites, on any terms sustainable. He saw clearly the inevitability of the white expansion with its never ending numbers and its burgeoning technology. To fight the whites would surely doom the people. In this, he proved true.

Black Kettle attended every peace conference he could and asked only that the whites tell him what the whites wanted of his people so that he could keep them out of harm's way. Consequently, his village was easy to find. In 1864, at Sand Creek in southern Colorado, his camp was surprised at dawn by the Colorado militia under the genocidal Chivington. Hundreds of women and children were maimed and murdered, and the village and its supplies burned.

Somehow Black Kettle managed to survive, but four years later, while encamped on the Washita in southern Oklahoma, on reservation lands set aside for the Cheyenne, his village was again surprised at dawn and again wiped out. This time Black Kettle was killed, his scalp carried away by mad dog white soldiers.

The Self Immolation of the Dogmen

Alone on Sappa Creek, in northwestern Kansas, the Dogmen waited for the arrival of a bluecoat column, known to be heading straight for their encampment. When the attack came, the small band disintegrated with scarcely any fight left in them.

Finally you run no more. You stay put and fight, no matter the odds or the inevitable outcome. To run away all the time, to constantly escape and avoid, is to effectively give up one's freedom. Better to die defending it than to live without it. Men can choose how they will live, even if only death proves it. Better to have chosen and suffer the consequences, than never to have chosen at all.

Dull Knife's Debacle

A similar resignation to ultimate fate took place in northern Wyoming, the winter after Custer's Last Stand. There, in the bitter cold of midwinter, another column of bluecoat calvary bore down on the village of Dull Knife. But instead of breaking camp and fleeing the path of the juggernaut, the Fox Soldiers decided the people would stay put. They surrounded the camp and forced all attempting to leave back to the lodges where they made the people dance and sing all night. At dawn the village was smashed, the remnants dragging into Crazy Horse's encampment several days later, half naked, frozen and starved.

That spring, Two Moons and a few bands surrendered in Montana. Dull Knife's and Little Wolf's people surrendered at Fort Robinson in northwestern Nebraska. But in the diddling, stupid way of the white fathers in Washington, instead of making a place for the Cheyenne among the Lakota as Dull Knife and Little Wolf had been led to believe, it was decided to ship them to southern Oklahoma to join the remnants of Black Kettle's people.

The Cheyenne resisted this idea, but in the end, Dull Knife and Little Wolf chose to be reasonable. They would go to the south and see for themselves what the whiteman offered there, believing that if they did not like what they saw they would have the right to return to their home in the north.

But when they arrived at the Oklahoma reservation, they were fed stinking food. Many got sick and died. In the infinite wisdom of Congress, no rations were budgeted for the Northern Cheyenne. They had to share the miserable allotments of the southern brethren. The children cried in hunger.

The Escape and Flight of a Thousand Perils

After a final diplomatic showdown with the Indian agent, Little Wolf and Dull Knife slipped their people out of camp right under the noses of the calvary under a full moon, and began the long impossible journey back to their homes in the north, straight across the now populated midsection of the country.

The Cheyenne fought running skirmishes with detachment after detachment of U.S. Calvary, escaping time and again, with half the country and the U.S. Army looking for and chasing after them, all two hundred and fifty of them, mostly women, children and old men. A masterful strategic and tactical feat, but like the rising drama of a Tolkein epic, the climax was still far away.

Once across the Platte, the two leaders split. Little Wolf's people would successfully hide out in the Sandhills through the winter and would finally reach Montana where they would surrender to the same soldier chief who had taken in Two Moons and his people.

Dull Knife's people were captured in a blizzard attempting to reach the Lakota at Red Cloud's Agency, and were incarcerated at Fort Robinson.

Again the mean spirited white fathers insisted that the Cheyenne go south. This time the Cheyenne adamantly refused. As punishment, they were confined to a barracks, 150 men, women and children, kept without heat or food for eight days. Denied even water for three.

The Final Massacre

Under an arctic cold full moon, this undefeated rabble broke out of the barracks, using the few guns their genius had hidden in pieces among the women and children. All fled into the cold ice night of hard death. The weak and the slow were shot down like dogs. Somehow Dull Knife and a few of his family escaped and made it finally to Red Cloud's lodge and succor. An extraordinary few made it up the sandstone buttes above the Fort, hiding out among the rocks and snow, fighting off the searching patrols, surviving for ten days, starting off with nothing at all except their freedom. The last of these were finally run to ground, holed up in exactly that, a hole they had dug out between a boulder and a rock ledge, killed in a suicide charge into volley after volley, three teenage boys and three teenage girls. A soldier is said to have exclaimed, "God, these people are hard to kill".

The love of freedom dies hard. The experience of freedom is incurable.

THE WARRIOR'S MIND

Living true freedom, despite its demands and uncertainties, is powerfully and psychologically reinforcing. The more you face its possibilities, the stronger you grow in response to its challenges. The more you enjoy its fruits, that quality of experience that grows within your bosom, the more satisfying life is. Nothing else can ever satisfy as much.

This effect comes at you both personally and socially. Personally, as you experience it as your self reliance. You get to know your independent, original nature and ability. You become original and able to feel good about yourself and the life you have, no matter its travails and pitfalls. Socially, a free people are a fun, energetic, open, productive, innovative and changing people. They stimulate, enjoy, reward, encourage, and challenge each other, yet they stay fair to each other and seek harmony among the people. You have to know and cherish freedom to grant it generously to all others. To live among a truly free and open people is a great fortune.

But such freedom is not license. Public observation and public response is an immediate, every day condition of tribal life. To share a culture of freedom is to share kinship among the people, all of whom have rights, dignities, and freedoms to personally enjoy. You can live free only by respecting the freedom of all others within the kinship, ideally including all humanity.

Such a culture of freedom, even with human imperfections, fosters the natural mind, the mind comfortable with its world as it truly is, the mind capable and ready to adapt, melding itself into the challenges of the real world as one undivided being, a mind that can feel the ferocity of the demon, and the kindness of the angel.

Only a mind that understands that only freedom holds its real fulfillment, that wonderful and mysterious river of human potential, only such a mind will defend that condition against all odds and danger, to where nothing matters but to live free or die.

THE WARRIOR'S HEART

We miss the water when the well runs dry. To enjoy freedom, its travails and its bounties, satisfies. We become keenly sensitive to the circumstances which produce this boon. One sees and feels that what is good should be kept good. But good fortune draws predators, and a free people always look a fresh resource to a diseased, presumptuous ruling class.

If a warrior cannot find the true courage in his heart to fight for the freedom of the people, as well as his own, he is a mere drone, a male whose only value is in the possibility that his seed mixed with woman might breed stronger men.

Deep courage cannot exist without deep motive. Money, promise of security, and ideological acceptance work for some men. Maybe most "civilized" males. All such motives are mercenary and shallow, for they occur for narrow, selfish reasons, without any consideration of the people, indeed, without any loyalty to the Law of Kinship. The strongest motive to fight comes from knowing that no other life is worth living.

The six indomitable Cheyenne teenagers who finished the epic tragedy of Cheyenne Autumn made enough weapons and clothes to have made a good start surviving a new life, and had killed and preserved a month's worth of meat to sustain them in the raw challenge of physical survival. They simply could not understand the possibility of exchanging this adversity for surrender to the sick white people who had imprisoned, starved, froze, and denied drink to women, children, and the innocent. They became very hard to kill. Surrender was not an option.

You cannot be dog soldier and not see, and know, what moved these young Cheyenne. Greater courage and fortitude is terribly hard to come by.

THE INEVITABLE APPEARANCE OF THE DOG SOLDIER

Genuine cultures of freedom breed competent, even great, warriors. The Cheyenne Dog Soldier and the American Ranger are not the only examples.

Shortly after the American Revolution stumbled its way to military victory, the slaves in Haiti revolted with a vengeance only the European Social Disease can spawn. While anarchy and barbarism reigned nearly everywhere, those who could protect their people, banded together in enough numbers to defy first the British, and then the Great Napoleon's armies, defeating them in detail, and remaining unconquered.

The greatest leader and general of these sudden warriors was Touissant L'Overture. An observer of his troops noted that they could run full out for 300 yards, dive to the ground, twisting and rolling like maddened snakes, firing their weapons faster than that managed by the well drilled European ranks of musketeers. Such maneuvers utterly broke up calvary charges.

By daring strategy, hard hitting tactics, by guile and clever retreat, Touissant L'Overture defied or defeated Europe's finest armies, the French and the British. But he became too noble at last, trusting the word of a French aristocrat, and was betrayed and taken prisoner. Giving one's word to a former slave, the inferior being, did not count to the Imperial European. Touissant died in a prison in France, a victim of the European Social Disease at its most ignoble.

Another telling case of the freedom bred warrior is that of the Boers of South Africa. Abandoned by the Dutch during the first British landgrab at Capetown, the Boers moved inland onto open plains and established the Orange Free State. When the British found that independence intolerable, they mounted several offensive campaigns against these new Boer homelands. They would subdue and properly subjugate the Boers, and pay for the effort in new tax collections.

Like the Cheyenne Dog Soldier and the American Ranger, the Boer warrior came out of the people, for they were one and the same as the people. Wonderfully, they combined the military strengths of both. They were mounted, self supplied, highly mobile, and great horsemen. They also wielded the long rifle with uncanny marksmanship. They could arrive on a flank, or a weak point, stand off at a distance, on horseback, out of range of the enemy's muskets, and enfilade the lines and ranks of the foe without mercy.

But Boer, like the dog soldier and th e ranger, had to return to the people to do the men's work of hunting, building, farming and harvesting. The welfare of the people depended upon them. The British, on the other hand, having the loot of an empire to feed their poor, breeding surplus males by the litter, could raise and advance still one more army of drones, and overwhelm by sheer mass of numbers and material, occupying the Boer lands at last, their men scattered across the plains keeping the people alive.

But the most compelling story belongs to William Wallace, and the common Scotsmen who rallied around him in rebellion against the cruelties, depredations and oppressions of the English overlords circa 1298 A.D. In one of the rare instances in European history, a commoner rose to become a great warrior chief, winning the hearts and minds of the people out from under the native aristocracy much to their consternation. Indeed, without the connivance and envy of his own nobility, Wallace would have won a lasting military supremacy based solely on the will and strength of the common people, a prospect no aristocrat would tolerate. In the end, Wallace was betrayed by his own "ruling class", captured, taken to London, publicly tortured, disemboweled, and finally beheaded. Taking the word of someone suffering from the European Social Disease is like petting a rattlesnake.

One can see the first glimmers of the Spirit of the American Revolution in Wallace's Rebellion.

In curious historical mimickery, Crazy Horse, a commoner who rose to be a great warrior chieftain of the Lakota, died a murderous death like Wallace, betrayed by his own "ruling class", physically held back by his once friend, and stabbed in the gut by bayonet. But the Scots, unlike the Lakota and Cheyenne, truly won their freedom in war a few years later at the Battle of Bannockburn, and had several hundred years to enjoy as an independent people. It was the Scottish economy that Adam Smith observed and admired while writing his landmark tome on free enterprise, published in 1776, the same year that Thomas Jefferson penned the Declaration of Independence.

Scots migrated to America, often and early, in far greater numbers then most realize. But they came in the modern condition, dispersed as individuals, north, south, seaboard and mountain. True, the English groomed Founding Fathers read John Locke, and understood revolutionary truths with sublime intellect. They were the brains of the American Revolution, this Great Experiment. But the Scots came with the living contagion of a long bred sense of freedom, dating farther back than even William Wallace, to the days when not even the mighty Romans could subdue them. Original, competent individuals, neatly interspersed throughout the frontier society, the common Scot was the cutting edge of the Revolution, the silver threads of well tempered freedom woven directly into the fabric of the American heart and soul.

THE MANUAL

MISSIONS

The mission of the Manual is to plant in the minds of those who study its contents an understanding and a belief that there is a greater purpose to human life than simply managing to live through it. Noble character is not a birthright. It must be won. If within each of us lies an embryonic spirit that can become great, it will only become great by disciplined cultivation, not by just going along with the flow, wherever that might lead.

Beyond this, the Manual offers a program of discipline for the dog soldier, not as sacred forms, rituals or immutable creed, but as only one vision of the dog soldier ideal. See how this illustration works, and then see what will work for you. Just remember, the discipline is not a set of beliefs, but a set of practices. With no practice, no effort, no self examination, there is no discipline, no cumulative effect. Any debate about beliefs becomes moot or immaterial. You cannot realize the fullest measure in the real and natural expression of the human spirit, your inner character and being, by knowing the truth. You must live and act in light of the truth. In a very real way, one does not actually master being a dog soldier, one simply becomes a dog soldier. This is what the doing and the discipline makes, dog soldiers, men you can ride the river with.

Individual destiny is the only true approach to human existence and personal experience. The species is flagrantly individual, original, and diverse. Mix these natural differences in with the vagaries of civilized fortune, where some are born rich and some are born poor, and you will find it difficult to identify two human beings that seem even remotely the same. Yet in each of the billions of unique mutations, every single one sees with the same kind of eyes, feels the same pangs and pleasures of the flesh, and experiences the same yearnings and stirrings of the heart. Each perceives and thinks with the same extraordinarily well equipped animal brain, and is capable of reflection, of learning, and intelligent behavior, even of defining moral conduct. Every human is conscious and as immersed in the human experience as all the rest. And all of us run the same risk of ending up in the long run maturity of adulthood quite empty inside, unhappy, rigid, and superfluous.

Living, mere survival amidst affluent material circumstances, is not enough. Neither is eating well, or sleeping on downy pillows. Doing all the apparent right things, career, marriage, offspring, retirement funds, is not enough. Neither is apparent success, to reach the heights of one's profession, or to suffer fame, profitable notoriety, or causal fortune. What matters is what drives the individual inside. Quality in human experience and existence comes from the inside out.

Real success and the right stuff follows from a deliberate process of conscious thought, purposeful action, and critical self examination. It is this process that forms our inner character. It is this process that cultivates the spirit until it knows itself. This is growth, and is what really matters most in living. Celebrity, fortune, idolatrous adulation, and the recounting of one's name among the legends of the people, these are not necessary results of the growth process. They are merely historical circumstances that coincide with the maturing, cumulative effects of a discipline of self betterment and personal growth. Their presence or absence weigh nothing in the balance of true inner character. What matters in the end is that you know where you have come from, and what you have finally become. Not even God can take that from you, or would wish to do so. Personal growth is the only meaningful purpose to human existence.

The mission of human life is to find and believe in the processes of self betterment, and once discovered, never cease to employ them. While the particulars of our personal fates may be mostly beyond our control, achieving a higher moral quality to our conduct and our being is a potential that exists in all humans. But it is only through our personal efforts that we even begin to reach the more noble, kind, and gracious selves we are all given the chance to become. God granted us the breath and the brains. But it is up to us to make something of that bounty. God gave us the spirit. But only we can give it greatness. If it doesn't come from us, it doesn't happen.

The dog soldier's discipline is simply this. Follow all your life a conscientious program of personal effort and self examination that breeds new growth, season after season, like the growth rings of a mighty tree. This cumulative, maturing inner growth becomes our moral strength and character. Nobility is found possible in all circumstances. Kindness is found possible in any situation. We exist on the wavecrest of one continuous present moment, lived directly and uncompromisingly through time, an ongoing volcanic eruption of the human spirit projecting itself into a cold, material universe, pushing out and on, sometimes for even a hundred years. How mighty is the oak at a hundred? How high is the volcano when the spirit moves on?

The dog soldier's life is intensely engaged in the human condition, day by day, scene by scene, alert, alive, intelligent and sensible, thoughtful and decisive. Through the positive discipline of process, the dog soldier grows with the seasons, in character and deed, in mind and spirit. This is the mission, the quest, the unprecedented journey of our personal lifetime. At any moment, we can discover what more a human can become, free to move spontaneously into the conduct of positive actions, the fulfillment of constructive purposes, and the creation of the good and the great that elevate the people beyond what they thought possible. All that without prospect or need for payoffs or applause, even when conditions are unfavorable and reality especially inclement. That is, when we need it most. The people never have too many dog soldiers among them.

For all this effort and striving, the final, well balanced inner dynamics realized in the mature dog soldier comes with two natural blessings. All present moments are enjoyable and renewing, and all one's deeds are meaningful and satisfying. Indeed, a conscientiously applied program of dog soldier discipline is like a healthy physical constitution. It is a robust defense against most of the debilitating ailments, dementias, and maladies that plague an unexamined, cluttered life. Rather, the more self reliant and self controlled you become, the less you experience the chronic worry, the brooding self pity, the petty angers and resentments, the nagging doubts, confused thought, and spiteful envy that leave the victim somewhere between the neanderthal and the Freudian neurotic. The maturing dog soldier is also less likely to fall into the big traps of modern life, the existential syndromes of angst, compulsive rigidity, schizoid personality, quiet desperation, emptiness, and the creeping stagnation that can arrive in the capstone years of human maturity and smother all future growth, even the breath of living itself.

In the final rendering, the dog soldier's mission is a direct expression of a genuine zest for life and a powerful drive to experience its further courses, directly and completely, as an original, free individual, whether or not such future proves boon or bane, or merely ordinary and mundane. The dog soldier lives without fear, for the spirit that grows also learns that it will endure. Free from the chains of the past, and knowing that whatever the future might hold, in opportunity or adversity, the dog soldier is ready to act, prepared to act, competent and confident, and firmly enmeshed in the future as it breaks open in the present, sure to grow another ring, whether defeat is suffered or success secured, or as most often happens, just another day in everyday human experience passing into memory, and the dawn of a new day waiting in the wings.

DOG SOLDIER CREDOS

To defend and protect the freedoms, rights and dignity of the people, the kinship, and all others within the shared society, especially those less able to defend those rights and freedoms themselves, the weak, the old, the children and the misfortunate.

To hate and fight against injustice and wrongdoing in any form at any time.

To despise deceit and hypocrisy, and those who prey upon the innocent and exploit the powerless, confronting and opposing them whenever and wherever encountered, righting wrongs and championing the true, the just, and the good.

To accept human nature and reality as they really are, and then to do what good can be done. No railing against the slings and arrows of outrageous fortune. It is all outrageous, the good and the bad. The truest act of defiance in an indifferent world is to survive, love life, and to grow in spirit, no matter the vicissitudes of fortune.

To be and do in a good, well meaning way toward others, kind in manner, noble in bearing, and genuine in conduct, so that the goodness spreads from one to another of the people, materially and morally, elevating them and giving them higher hopes.

To do good works freely, from giving encouragement to others to providing real material assistance to those in need, making a stronger people, and a healthier one, through example, through honor, and through direct conduct, making each day of living worthwhile and better, for oneself and for the kinship.

PROCESS

Dog soldier discipline is an ever working process in pursuing real objects. What matters is how the one's behavior actually works in the real world, that is, to what effect do one's actions run, on nature, one's self, and on others. What doesn't matter is how one's actions look or conform to any a priori creed, inherited codes, or specious ideologies. One can easily adopt programs of discipline and simply end up going through the motions, with no noticeable outcome worth mentioning. Without true understanding of the process between ends and means, self improvement is accidental, if it occurs at all.

The central struggle in the dog soldier discipline lies between the demands of undivided, intelligent presence, genuinely engaged in the pursuit and the progress toward real changes in one's conduct, attitude and being, and the degradation of this endeavor into rule following behavior, the observance of forms, that habituation to routine without thought, where concentration and focus is on forms prescribed, programmed, and accordingly conformed to. The human being comes with considerable strengths and maddening imperfections. We can build and drive cars, and still we fall asleep at the wheel. It is always easy for the human to lose sight of the whys involved in what we do, and quit measuring the presence of real effects as once envisioned. We slip into just doing this or that because we have formed a habit, simply programming ourselves to do the thing on cue, without reference to purpose, or effects, or benefits realized. All that matters in rule following behavior is that the action be performed on schedule, that the motions conducted are properly executed as prescribed, and that the completion of the duty be duly noted.

A mind and body so dominated by the rule following mindset results in odd, elderly male joggers. You can spot them about anywhere, all sportswear correct, moving arms and joints all about in tiny, exaggerated swings that never vary, springing forward in an accentuated shuffle, maybe six inches a step. Their faces beam with the effort consumed in the rigors of physical conditioning as they slowly break the crest of the hill. All muscle, ligament, tendon and bone are vigorously rubbed and ground in exactly the same way, at exactly the same points, again and again with gusto. Yet the horse power exertion in this ginger assault upon gravity is hardly tenth of what a best efforts striding gait would exact, where arms and frame all swing broadly to increase the throw of momentum forward into the next stride. If the object is to work out the body fully and to incite the heart to push itself into a warm cardiac burn, a true strolling walk, well paced, would far better achieve these ends then would the martinet pigeon steps of the aging jogger drone. Process keys on function and reshapes itself as effects are perceived. This is feedback. No feedback, no process. Rule following behavior keys on form and perfect itself for its own sake. The feedback loop is disconnected. No reshaping takes place.

Unfortunately, one of the necessary requirements for defining function is the use of specific forms to illustrate the concept, so form must be indulged. But the Manual is about objects, the pursuit of which must be functionally driven, with form free to vary. The point is to see and keep one's eye on the objectives, and to discern the truth of progress and good effect. What fulfills the object is useful and valid. What does not is a waste of time.

This is the point of discipline. To select behaviors for repetition because their evident effects allign with the end in view. Useless, inconsequential, or ineffectual behaviors are dropped from practice.

The general process to apply in all realms of self conditioning is simple. Pay attention to what you do and the effects that come from what you do against the objectives you have set for yourself. Then judge the worth of those results against given the costs and effort spent. Finally, move to adjust future your practice and conduct in accordance with what you learn. Progress in human affairs often comes only a tablespoon at a time. But over the long run of one's life, you can fill the ocean.

An excellent illustration in what the Manual can do and what the reader must supply can be found in the business of teaching a young pitcher how to throw a curve ball. You can show them how to grip the ball, the spinning action you must impart, and the point of release required, but they must throw the ball. They are the ones who must develop a comfortable position for the ball in their hands. They are the ones who must find the inner feelings and senses that define the execution of the twisting, whipping action of the arm and wrist. They must, by performance, actually release the ball at some point, marking the body memory to find that point again. The pitcher who finally learns and masters the curve is the one who can see for themselves the truth of the effort in the flight of the ball, does the pitch break or not?

Focus on the objectives. See the truth of your efforts, their effects on your living. You will seldom find yourself in perfect imitation of your ideals. Process is more a matter of keeping a firm hand on the keel and holding the heading on course than it is of final formal attainment. Remember that knowing is not enough. You have to perceive, move, observe, learn, and move again. The only time process fails is when you quit.

THE VENUES OF SELF BETTERMENT

The ultimate venue of self betterment is simply your life, in all its outward and inward aspects. Outwardly, the venues are the scenes and settings found where you live, work, shop, and play, that is, all the places you inhabit or frequent. Often these outward venues come loaded with people, some close, some strangers, many with whom you will interact, relate, or simply exist together with, at the same place in the same present time. Inwardly, the venues are the mind and heart of your conscious experience, your thinking and your feeling. Together, the public and the private, make up your total natural existence as a surviving human being.

Not every one of these settings or scenes you live through and experience will be an occasion for dramatic insights, defining moments, or exemplary deeds. In fact, most will not. Life is ordinary first. Self betterment is more of a seeping process. To be a little more aware of what is going on around. To be a little more genuine when holding a door open for some one. To be a little quicker to give, or accept, to smile, or just be friendly. To be a little surer and more apt to move spontaneously to do a decent thing, a more intelligent thing, or just a useful, good thing. Most of the confirming instances of the presence of our character occur in these many common, everyday vignettes that run together in the living river of presence and experience that is essentially who we are and will be as a human being.

This is the payoff self betterment seeks, the whole point of the dog soldier process. To make changes in yourself that change how you will project yourself into in all the future venues of your life, responding in that place, at that time, as well or better than you had done in handling similar circumstances in the past. For there is opportunity in every venue, every scene, for actions that embody virtue and finer conduct. When you begin to see those opportunities and to act upon them positively, then the cumulative effects of the disciplined process are beginning to show.

The expression of character and all growth in character occurs in venue. The process of self betterment takes and becomes self sustainable when you sense and perceive these cumulative effects in your presence and behavior as you progress through the days and weeks of your life. You see that you are acting and feeling in new ways, and better more often than not. Positive happenings and finer satisfactions feedback into the belief and the effort. You discover that the seeds of growth and the fulfillment of character exist in every act you perform, in every feeling you experience, wherever you might be along the journeys and seasons of your life. It is as if the roots of spirit sink deeper and a new energy in conscious experience nourishes your will and being as never before. Eventually you can live no other way. Like the Cheyenne. Your loyalty to virtues and ideals, and your growth in the character they shape, define you, renew you, and finally are you, a work of art and purpose a lifetime in the making. Hard to kill. There is no final attainment to a living process, only its end in death.

Character can only be measured by its projection into our behavior in the real scenes and settings of human existence. You may talk a good game, or like the Pharisee, plead perfection of form, but if you miss the opportunities latent in every venue you travel through, your claims and your efforts are in vain. Don't just be there. Do something while you are there.

SEVEN WORTHY VIRTUES

Seven worthy virtues to be sought and cultivated in oneself, and admired and honored in others, are honesty, bravery, fortitude, generosity, fairness, endeavor, and wisdom. Each are hard to acquire and even harder to keep. Much easier to go with the flow and rationalize later that one's conduct was virtuously inspired.

But when virtue and ideals shape your conduct, when their presence in character is confirmed in your behavior, the result is a sense of integrity and dignity that is deep and palatable. This inner fulfillment of spirit can be got no other way. The Manual is not about sainthood. The contribution of the warrior lies in other ways. But the progressions of changes in conscious experience that emerge and mature in the saint are like the changes that come with dog soldier discipline. In the end, you are changed, and find that much to the better. At some point, the process is irreversible. Once original, always original.

Honesty

Honesty is to act and speak with integrity, free of fraud. To be straightforward and upright in conduct and thought. To be genuine, open, frank, and conscientious. To be scrupulously truthful, objective and candid.

Above all, honesty is to be consistent between inside and out, free of hypocrisy. Neither should the honest man allow misperceptions to stand, letting others believe that we think or feel a certain way when we do not, leaving the error uncorrected in their minds. Nor should untruths said about others be allowed to stand. Acquiescence in lies is as degrading as the lies.

Honesty does not require a compulsion to invariably confess the truth. Freedom is nothing without privacy, for ourselves and others. Others do not need to hear everything we have to tell about ourselves. Nor should they be expected to indulge us should we try. Neither is bluntness especially called for. There are many ways to communicate the truth, many indirect. Sometimes the most honest response is silence.

The contrary vices to honesty are lying, mendacity, deceit, hypocrisy, fraud and phoniness.

Bravery

Bravery is to act courageously and without fear. To be dauntless and intrepid when confronting adversity. To be bold and daring in the face of challenge. Bravery will also confront rude behavior, oppose misconduct, resist wrong doing, and fight evil and injustice.

Right actions and honorable conduct in comfortable settings and easy circumstances are like setting sails to a full wind. They are worthy but not especially difficult. What distinguishes the heroic and the noble is their appearance in ill winds, in the presence of danger and the prospects of personal sacrifice. Invariably, the time arrives when the actions and conduct most needed, most demanded by character, must occur in conditions that are adverse, discouraging, or frightening. We sense the danger like any animal, and sensibly seek to stay out of harm's way. We secretly give into fear and rationalize our actions away. Some things are hard to do. But only these are the true challenges. Courage, bravery, these are the inner forces that move us to overcome fear and accomplish the good and the great when they are most difficult and most needed.

The contrary vices to bravery are cowardice, timidity, lethargy, and apathy.

Fortitude

Fortitude is strength to carry on over the long run, to be tenacious in seeing things through to their ends. To show firmness of mind and resolute endurance in meeting danger, adversity, or in fulfilling a purpose. Fortitude combines courage and staying power, and is called many things by the Americans, grit, backbone, pluck, guts, sand, and gumption.

Fortitude will not be downed by difficulties or hardship, and willingly suffers the privation, pain, and sacrifices necessary to reach one's goal. Fortitude will fight and continue fighting against great odds, and shows physical and mental vigor when facing things which repel or frighten. Fortitude also means holding to one's principles even at cost to oneself.

The contrary vices to fortitude are timidity, faint heartedness, laziness, and giving up.

Generosity

The giving of generosity is expressed both materially and morally. It is a fullness of spirit that gives freely, infused with a magnanimous nature that is exuberant, benevolent, and openhanded. Generosity shows a friendly liberality in one's actions toward others, sharing richly and completely, for the goodness of feeling that it creates in all.

There is a seldom tested theory that the more you give away, the more it all comes back to you, and then some. Perhaps modern society is a poor testing ground, but to be able to share freely and without reservation with others in need proves an underlying sense of completeness in the life and character of the giver. Rather than diminish one's real wealth, generosity invest it in others. Rather than hording beyond one's real needs, generosity shares it where it will make a real difference elsewhere. Rather than dividing society into rich and poor, generosity reaffirms that we are one common people.

The contrary vices to generosity are stinginess, meanness, ignoble and miserly conduct, rude behavior, narrow mindedness, greed, bigotry, and envy.

Fairness

Fairness is to be frank, honest, upright and just in one's dealings with others. To speak with candor and to act without prejudice. To be equitable and impartial in judging others or making judgements.

How you treat others is the acid test of character. How the various people treat each other is the acid test of society. A just society lives on fairness and due process. There is no other way a just society is possible. Even the smallest child has a keen sense of fairness. They see and acutely feel differential treatment between what befalls them and the boons that befall others. We can take some variance in fortune and prospects, but there is a threshold beyond which no human sensibly human could countenance or tolerate without degradation. A tolerance of unfairness in their favor is the most virulent toxin at work when people succumb to the European Social Disease, its malignance, a spreading unhappiness among the people. A society based on unfairness ends in the caste system and dies. A society based on freedom and fairness stays alive and matures.

The contrary vices to fairness are partiality, injustice, bias, prejudice, unfairness, cheating, calumny, bigotry, self superiority, vanity, and arrogance.

Endeavor

Endeavor is first to have purposes, useful projects to complete, adventures to take, goals to achieve. Endeavor then becomes the effort and the striving, the work undertaken and performed to reach the end in view. Endeavor is the resolve to apply oneself, to struggle against distractions and failures until accomplishment is realized. Endeavor takes pains. If one is to do a thing, they should do it well.

The human spirit needs to achieve. Why else are we given a nature that thrives on progressive accomplishments, a nature that pushes the envelope even when we are pushing eighty. We gain satisfaction and reinforcement from each accomplishment our plans and efforts produce, whether we lay up wood enough for winter, build a better rat trap, or stay a course we have put before ourselves. Endeavor is the driver of all growth for it places us at risk. Sometimes we succeed, but often we do not. So we learn. Human intelligence is a dynamic process. It pushes and prods us into smarter directions. It finds better, more effective ways to do about anything. But first intelligence must have something to work with, experience. This is what endeavor supplies, experience. When you move, you find things out. Always be about doing things, and you will find that life draws you along quite nicely, like a current favors a firm hand on the keel.

Contrary vices to endeavor are laziness, indolence, listlessness, purposeless existence, and comatose chairs.

Wisdom

Wisdom is the ability to judge matters soundly, to deal sagaciously with the facts as they relate to life and conduct. Wisdom is foresighted, yet cautious, circumspect and calculating, shrewd, astute, and knowing. Above all, wisdom is sensible and sane. A wise man will be discerning in their understanding of persons, conditions, and situations, and will know how to deal with them, correct what is wrong in them, and to be able to get the best out of people and circumstances, given the natural limitations and difficulties of reality. Wisdom estimates fairly and accurately, makes thoughtful decisions, and reaches just conclusions. Even among good men, things go wrong. Wisdom catches such mishaps and sets them straight.

When applied to one's self, wisdom keeps oneself, one's passions and actions, under control, and in obedience to what one knows is right and necessary. The wise man is level headed and even tempered.

The rhythm of wisdom is patience. So much can change with the passage of time. Mountains become molehills, new conditions wipe away present worries. Perhaps the highest art of wisdom is knowing when not to judge, when not to decide, and when not to act.

Contrary vices to wisdom are stupidity, ignorance, folly, narrow mindedness, foolishness, fixation, prejudice, bigotry, close mindedness, self righteousness, blind meanness.

THREE CULTURES

Culture is all the learned ways of a people, their customs, practices, and technologies, refined by experience over the lifetimes of the people, and passed on, indeed bred into the next generation, by conscious, common, and concerted efforts, so that they can carry on society without losing ground.

But living a culture is an individual affair, where personal choices and efforts combine to create some cumulative effect in the individual. Whether we employ craft, purpose, and discipline in conduct, or let the flow do it for us, there is always cumulative effect to our choices and the patterns of behavior we engage in. It all adds up, whether we pay attention or not.

The reason the wise in all cultures throughout history have found value in governing one's actions by principle is because principle concentrates the effects of our choices and deeds. This concentration leads to positive changes in how we think, feel. Things go better with principle. To set for yourself an ideal, perhaps as simple as to say "thank you" readily, or perhaps as difficult as the Golden Rule, is to make it a part of your personal culture, to choose it as part of the fabric of your character, fully present in your everyday living. Three powerful ideals of dog soldier culture are freedom, truth, and character.

Like all objects of personal change, the self enculturation of an ideal is a process. One begins with a studied apprehension and appreciation of what makes up the ideal. Then with deliberate purpose and self discipline, one breeds this governance into one's conduct where it works to shape our inner character. This is cultivation. To bring out and nurture the better sides of ourselves.

The Culture of Freedom

Freedom is such a basic condition of natural human existence that it is ironic and rather sad that it is so hard to come by and keep in "civilized" societies. It is as if we do not really trust freedom. Invariably, our contrivances at a body politic, even those with the most sweeping charters of human freedom, end up seeking to qualify personal rights and freedoms with petty restrictions, police state sanctions, and politically correct propaganda, far beyond what is necessary to assure an orderly society. Government as it grows long in the tooth increasingly attempts to mircromanage the personal choices of the people. Its tools are myriads of legislation, defining transgression upon transgression, each backed by the bludgeoning punishments of the state and its overwhelming powers of execution. Hard to trust the common man if you think you are superior.

If you say you choose freedom, then you must give up the idea of controlling other people's personal choices and accept what liberty spawns. Order must come from the people themselves, as they confront each other other's actions and appetites in the concourses of the free environment. Our freely formed enterprises with each other, because of the common interest, shape order out of what would seem a recipe for anarchy. Freely spoken opinions and shared speech form shared understandings even in the presence of disagreements. We learn how to live and let live. The societal discipline that is needed is provided by a positive discipline that comes from within each individual of the people. This is the only sure basis of society anyway, even in a police state. In a culture of freedom, positive discipline flourishes. So do its failures. There will always be someone who will walk into the Grand Canyon because someone forgot to post a sign.

Inner discipline and character formation are the natural consequences of cultures of freedom. When facing challenge and adversity, free to choose, you have to decide matters for yourself. You must draw on inner resources to guide your choosing. There the consequences of your decision must be borne, inside, where only you know the truth. No freedom, no inner consequences, no breeding. If efficient outward conformity is all that matters, one gets by and nothing more is asked.

The primal drive behind the insuppressible urge to live free is the never dying sense that knows that freedom is the only proper, and the most fulfilling, condition of existence for the human spirit. Material affluence without freedom makes a better dressed chimpanzee, but leaves the human spirit malnourished and undeveloped. The true source of inner character lies in the risks of freedom. Nothing else stimulates the spirit to grow.

Over history, humans have adapted to the most godawful circumstances, even Aushwitz, but even the most broken down slave knows and feels what it means to be free. Were slavery or coerced conformity good for the human spirit, the slave and the drone would be content. They would feel no other life is desirable. They would not dream to be free. But something yearns inside, and finally rebels or dies. We were meant to grow like the great oak far out on the prairie, not like a stunted bonsai bush stuck in a pot.

Essential to establishing a sustainable culture of freedom is recognizing that freedom must be reciprocal. We each have a right to our natural freedom, but we can only surely enjoy it to the extent that we extend, recognize and respect the same in all others. To think others should act, think, and behave a certain way, especially with you as the arbiter, and to hold against them their nonconformity and noncompliance, irrevocably violates the Rule of Reciprocity. To coerce, threaten, force or punish others for not being like us, violates the very essence of human freedom. This is the European Social Disease and its coercive culture of hierarchical conformity. If you have no real choice, you have that much less freedom.

A culture of freedom demands self reliance in the individual in the face of risk and uncertainty. It believes such prospect is possible in all humans, even if some fail. A culture of freedom also trusts the people to work out civil order amongst themselves. If some of the results present in modern socity seem discouraging, it is not for want of knowing how to better. Were the Golden Rule of Tolerance, "Live and let live", and the Golden Rule of Conduct, "Do unto others as you would have done unto yourself", better observed, a just and still free society would seem easy to attain and to keep. If you cannot trust freedom in the people, then you do not trust the people.

But to have freedom is not enough. One must drink it in deeply before one can fulfill their human potential, that of becoming an original individual. Freedom without adventure or discovery exploring its ranges, pushing hard against the envelope, is a passive, inert condition, not a real freedom at all. If one does not live free, no blather of words, spoken or written in law, offer any compensation for the loss.

If one does not engage in the quests, journeys, and enterprises of freedom, one wears the balls and chains of self imposed limits, a slave to one's own timidity. A life of freedom means challenge, uncertainty and adversity. But it is the foundation of dignity and character, for it tests the individual, bringing success and bringing failure, both which temper and strengthen the spirit.

If you want great warriors, keep the people free.

The Culture of Truth

All worlds run better on truth, personal, social, and material. A culture of truth is not just a matter of telling the truth, of honesty. The ideal is to seek, know, and understand the truth about one's self, other people, and the real world, and then accept it and work from there. The dog soldier must be realistic in their planning and expectations. Living truth means always observing the real facts. This is the only way one can intelligently change one's ways and means in meeting ends and fulfilling purposes.

Truth makes a stronger mind and a freer one. One can easily become a slave to one's lies and self delusions, anxiously spending much time and effort trying to keep them straight and undetected. Indifference in knowing the truth of things makes life more uncertain, confusing and more difficult than it need be. Wanton disregard for the truth makes life insane. Correspondingly, living a culture of truth also means defending the truth, even fighting for it, against all lies, especially the big ones.

Finally, the culture of truth demands character, for while the truth may set us free, sometimes it hurts. A confrontation with truth can sometimes be as bruising as an unwanted tumble on the ice. But the body heals and you get a little wiser for the fall. Eventually, truth makes for a stabler and stronger emotional life, for one lives without delusion. With the truth, one can feel the steady currents of reality deeply without interference. When one sees the truth as it is and accepts it, one is not easily perturbed.

The Culture of Character

Human life consists of many proving trails, one after another, and often several at once. We are not born to character, though the foundation and potential exists within all of us. Character grows and takes shape, if it appears at all, in a steady, accumulating way, through our experiences with adversity and opportunity, through good fortune and bad. Character is put to the test, and thus tempered, when conditions change on us, when our plans and expectations are thwarted, held back, or derailed.

Character develops out of how we finally take our experience, the good, the bad, and the ugly. Even apparent success is no guarantor of growth in character. Fortune smiles on some and not on others. Some of the success experienced by individuals will happen no matter what their strategy or its execution. Fools have stumbled into wealth and power, though they are seldom allowed to keep it.

The culture of character begins with the idea that character must be built up over time, that lessons are to be learned in all events and situations, and that deliberately placing one's self on proving trails confronts the truth of one's character and sets the stage for its advancement. We grow in character, first by trying, and then by trying to do better.

More than all other cultures, character requires honest self examination, hard judgement, and a stern resolve to live and behave in new ways, even harder ways, in accordance with what one comes to believe are the right ways, the just ways, the best ways. Character is loyal to the obligations one sets for one's self and does not easily give them up. What the many say, what the few rave, is largely incidental.

Good character is the triumph of one's sense of honor. We experience this as dignity. When we fail to grow in character, we squander our human potential, our birthright to become more than we are. Without character in the people, a just society is not possible. Unless the moral sense is internalized in the many, no expressions of morality in law can make up the difference.

THE OBJECTS OF DISCIPLINE

If you practice, prepare, even measure progress, it must be toward some end in view. These ends in view are the objects of discipline. They are the real, lasting changes that we seek to achieve in ourselves, our conscious experience, and our behavior. The apprehension of the difference these changes can make in us is what inspires and motivates discipline. The possibility of the change, and the worth of its benefits, must be perceived to be real. How can anyone strive for what they cannot envision?

Discipline is too often misunderstood as its caricature, rule following behavior. The "disciplined" person has it all down to the timetable and never fails their quota. Such determination is the start of good discipline, but it must mature into the understanding that both the objects and means of discipline themselves might merit change. The world changes. We age. The demands and needs of the season must be met. There will be a constant stream of feedback to take into account, and a continual redefinition of the objects of discipline to pursue.

The Manual divides all objects of discipline, the far beacons of self betterment, into three braod categories. All objects pertaining to our human nature are considered matters of personal grooming. This includes the core set of mental, physical, and emotional objectives for the dog soldier. Objects pertaining to our animal nature are animal matters, things like hair, feeding, habitats, and physical tensions. Objects pertaining to our social nature are our worldly affairs, government, culture, manners and conduct, and the like.

In all areas of conditioning, there is one general method you should follow. Focus on the objectives, the ends in view, the needs to be satisfied, or the benefits to be gained. Pay attention to what you do and the results you observe. Trust your native intelligence and let your practices evolve. As you gain experience, this, too, will guide you. Paying attention, native intelligence, and experience are what make up the elusive common sense.

Personal Grooming

All things that stimulate, shape, and sustain strong and sound minds, good and brave hearts, strong and supple bodies, and rugged, robust constitutions, are matters of personal grooming and hygiene. The combined and cumulative effect of these practices is what we call sound personal health, a health involves that permeates all dimensions we associate with the whole being, mental, physical, and emotional. Other topics covered under personal grooming are spirituality, expressiveness, and personal presence.

The challenge is simple. You have human brains. Can you learn how to use them? Can you learn how to take care of yourself well? Can you use your brains to propel you into the undiscovered country of self betterment, no matter how small the victories. Self reliance begins in all of us as a simple, common drive to be responsible for ourselves. Learning how to cultivate what you are, what you want to be, and what you can be for the better, is really all the human experience is about.

Physical Conditioning

The human animal is made to be in motion. We come alive when we move. We climb trees, look around corners, run long distances, lift and carry heavy loads, swim rivers, throw objects with accuracy, and ascend high mountains just to get a good look around before we decide where we will go next. Any natural ability if employed is satisfying and reinforcing. When normal circumstances in work and living do not afford much latitude in physical expression, we invent athletic games and play them. The psychosomatic connection is real. A robust physical exuberance in living is the foundation of a sound, healthy, resilient mind.

There are three objects to physical conditioning, strength, endurance, and agility.

Strength is the sheer muscle force one can deliver in carrying out a physical feat. Most modern programs of strength development are narrow, building strength in right angle actions. But strength is needed in all the many positions and postures the body may find itself in, and throughout all their many angles of leverage. The real world demands on our strength come at us in all manner of geometry and dynamics. Swinging and moving about a light barbell, holding odd positions and testing various twists and turns, can stand one in better stead then doubling or tripling one's naturally given strength in narrow, restricted motions that the real world seldom presents any occasion for employment.

Endurance is staying power in the face of prolonged physical demands. It is the second wind, a strong heart, and a dogged stamina in finishing what has been begun. Endurance, like strength, can be conditioned along forms too narrow. What is wanted is an endurance across many diverse kinds of physical activity, not just one.

Agility is the swift and sure movement from one physical position or motion to another. The key to agility, its quickness and its grace, is stretching and limbering the muscles and joints through all the motions their architecture permits and makes possible. The physical demands of real world action do not come in predictable, easy forms. The physical response that makes the difference may be one that you would never encounter in the safe confines of everyday behavior.

Though Tai Chi is thought to be an exercise designed only for the elderly Chinese, limbering routines that match its diversity of form, rhythm, and sudden motion, exercise the agility that should be present in our expressions of physical grace and prowess.

There are two principles to employ in guiding your program and discipline of physical conditioning, cross train and push the envelope.

Mix up your activities in pursuit of each objective. The human body is designed for an incredible range of whole body motion, from the skilled and aggressive, to the graceful and the beautiful. The net result of your set of physical conditioning behaviors should be that every muscle is worked and stretched, every ligament and tendon tested, and every joint taken through all its available angles. Through all this is the hidden conditioning, that of the nervous system's control and command of any motion you choose or need to make. All this creates a well rounded balance in physical prowess, and is usually more adaptive and productive than overdeveloped proficiency in narrow ranges.

An excellent example of this principle is the classic calisthenic set. Though no longer in vogue in the era of personal trainers and fitness machines, vigorously completing the calisthenics routine exercises the body in many different motions, angles and postures.

And from time to time, push the envelope. Find the boundaries of your physical competence and press them. The sudden physical demands reality might thrust upon you will do this for you, prepared or not. So do it in your own conditioning. Not all the time. But understand the rhythms of exercise and physical activity, between the light work and the demanding. Unless you truly push on your limits, and find yourself drawing yourself up to gather another wind, how will the brain know where to direct its physiological response to your effort. No pain, no aches, no struggle, no weariness, no improvement in your physical condition.

Grace and Prowess

We are stuck with the physical nature our genetic makeup gives us. Humans come in many variations in bone structure, body type, shape, and size, only a few combinations of which are ideally suited for the classic physical feats of the species, disk throwing, running, jumping, catching passes, or hitting a golf ball. Of our imperfections, our physical ones are the most glaring.

But no matter how we think we win or lose the physical specimen lottery, we can develop what we have. Each human can find easy grace in all their movements, large and small, those endless motions that make the river of behavior for the day. Each human can take what actions and skills they must daily perform, and learn how to do them with more effectiveness and more efficiency, that is, with grace and ease.

Too often the ends of physical conditioning are seen as only a strong heart, a sturdy constitution, and stress reduction. But if the effects of your physical conditioning do not show themselves in a growing gracefulness in your motions, and in a growing prowess in all your necessary actions, something is not working right.

Grace is a body tuned to its physical sense of presence, one comfortable at rest or in motion, ready to move easily and with pleasing appearance. Prowess is increasing efficiency and effectiveness in getting done what needs to be done. These ends to physical conditioning, grace and prowess, are just as important as the long beating heart. Why live long if it is to be as dull and ploddish as it ever was?

Physical Expression

The voice and face are just as worthy of physical conditioning as are the bones and muscles. Much of personal presence comes from a cultivated voice and a well versed face. Study the animal in the mirror even if you do not have a mirror. Growl, snarl, hiss and howl. Smile, turn serious, look patient and laugh. Sing in the shower at the top of your lungs in all the strange ranges of your voice. You will find that attention and practice increases the range and sharpness of your facial expressions and gives your voice a new power, just as surely as attention and practice work to make you stronger, quicker, and more agile.

Look at the faces around you in public. Many can be observed in pristine moments driving cars around on the streets. You will begin to note the sorry record of modern "civilization", faces clamped tight, permanent frowns and snarls, the clenched jaws, the carved in crossness, the sour-pusses and bitter mouths, and the just plain mean looking faces. Or the other scary variety, the blank, caved in looks, the worry worn, the scared, frozen faces, and the dried up, unmoving ones. When spotted in the elderly, it is especially sad, enough to discourage the unborn from ever wanting a human life.

The hands and the body are also important ingredients in physical expression. The hands talk and the body tells. Their language is the rhythm of music and dance. Spend time with music and practice what the hands can say and do, and how the body moves to carry them through. Flamboyant gestures are not necessary. But you want your hands and body to show more life than the monotonous cadaver motions some men bring along to social occasions.

We all develop our own styles of expression, as fits our temperament, what psychologists call personality. The object in conditioning our expressive nature is not to make all flamboyant and extroverted. What you want is a face that in later age, when in repose, looks like a face that has been comfortably in motion all its life, capable of moving decidedly into clearly understood expressions. There is a repertoire of expression just as there is a repertoire of physical motion. It only makes sense to develop that as well, to the point where you are intuitively in command of what your face, hands, and voice tells others.

Mental Conditioning

Mental conditioning is a far more diversified proposition than physical conditioning. Virtually any mental skill or ability you pick up and develop can contribute in some way over the long run to the quality of your mental life. But these beneficial effects from mental conditioning, a sound, sharp, strong mind, can be quite elusive. If you carry out the motions of a program of physical conditioning, you get the effect. There is no such guarantee with the mind.

The difficulty arises from the fact that while we see and are directly aware of our physical behavior, we live on the face of our minds looking out, and are therefore, far less aware or cognizant of the underwriting mental processes our consciousness breaks out from. Then, even when we are aware, the complexity possible in mental life allows us to lie to ourselves about what we are aware of.

Being honest with yourself in the observation and cultivation of your mind is a necessary precondition to effective mental conditioning. You have to know what you know, and know what you don't know. You have to look at a thought, or a feeling, and see it as it really is. If you allow yourself to revise in your mind your perceptions of its workings, pretending they are something else, you cannot improve your mind.

Otherwise, the same general rules for self conditioning apply. Pay attention to what is going on in your mind, its workings, its awarenesses, its hang ups and pitfalls. Then trust your native intelligence, learn something, and guide your future thinking in accordance with what you learn.

What you want to discover and keep is the natural mind, a mind well versed, well reposed and practiced, one ready to respond spontaneously and rationally to the breaking events of natural reality. Throughout the progress of the day's many chores and situations, the natural mind is an focused, undivided mind, keyed on the present moment, no Freudian Underground lurking. In the porcess, the whole quality of your conscious experience undergoes a metamorphosis. In the paradoxical dynamic of human growth, we become something more and different from what we were, and eventually forget what was once the poorer nature of our conscious life. We change in whole being, and live there looking forward to more.

But to reach the natural mind, you have to teach yourself to closely observe the workings of your own mind, and see that you can intervene and gradually shape the progression of your mental living for the better. In his famous old age, Socrates said, "Know thyself. The unexamined life is not worth living." Living without self examination is to fail the human potential.

Education

Even in the relatively simple society of the tribe, the number or things that a child must learn to become a competent adult is enormous, how to act, how to be, how to do, in the dozens of odd personal and social situations that pass for a day in a human life. Every adult in the kinship was expected to help. In modern society, a large share of this great responsibility is placed with the institutions of formal education, especially the chore of teaching the keystone literacy and technological skills that unlock the vast storehouses of modern knowledge. Acquiring an expertise or economic viability through formal education is a sensible goal for anyone. But formal educational processes should also change the way you see, think, and reason. Even if poorly taught, the opportunity to read and see how the great minds of history thought and wrote, teaches the open mind the ways of rational thinking. A sluffing, capricious attitude towards one's education is more befitting the chimpanzee than the human.

But there is much more to the education of a man than formal schooling. Reality is many faceted, and portentous. People and their behavior astonish and intrigue us. We ask questions without words in our minds, and wonder about answers. When we concentrate our questioning, and actively acquire and think through the facts of a matter, we study the matter. And somehow, in the end, we decide something that gives us a better grasp as to what the matter is about. Self study is the habit of mind that cultivates wisdom. A dog soldier's self education should be a daily and a life long affair.

Unless somehow beaten or discouraged out of people, a natural curiosity and an absorbing capacity to be interested, is a vibrant part of the human makeup. Like any natural motivation, its employment is satisfying and reinforcing. The learning behaviors of self study are uncomplicated. Read, ask, observe, listen, and then think things through to their ends. Organize the knowledge in your mind and search for its applications. Understand what you do not know as keenly as what you think you know. Informing ourselves and judging for ourselves, this is the stuff of a free mind.

A free thinker is an independently motivated, ever learning, a self reliant thinker. There are many worldly things to know about, many useful skills one can acquire and learn to perform to good effect. The knowledge works to extend our awareness and comprehension of what life in this universe is, and the skills work together to secure our personal well being, what makes us self reliant. Especially of value is the set of personal skills that keep you together as a physical animal, be it cooking, ironing, changing a tire, tending a cold, or sleeping better.

But the most prized skill of the dog soldier is rationality.

Rationality

The many indigenous paradigms of rational thought are essentially the expression of the tool maker's bent in the workings of the conscious mind. We identify and keep to patterns of conscious phenomena that improve our understanding of the real world, and aid us in the actions we undertake within our environment to provide for our well being. This is no different in principle from what the concrete tool provides when we apply it to operate upon the environment to some productive end. Both rational thought and the tool provide a characteristic range of outcomes that are reliable and instrumental in how well we deal with the environments in which we must adapt and survive. Being rational is simply using our native intelligence with deliberation.

The bottom line of rational behavior is the weighing equation. We weigh costs and benefits between choices, evaluate the pro's and con's of a strategy, or tally up like Benjamin Franklin, the pluses and minuses between effort and outcome. Sometimes we are aided by objective method, but in most daily affairs, we must rely on native intuition guided by experience. The idea is to make the best choice, or at least a good one. We look at the consequences to tell us how well we did. But as we learn which modes of apparent rationality really work, as we become more effective in our thinking, we tend to stay rational all the time, and simplify our lives so much more. One can waste an inordinate amount time wallowing in the mishaps of dumb behavior.

The greatest nemesis to rational human behavior, apart from blind attitudes, rat trap fixations, and Freudian dementias, is the failure to think things through to their ends. This is largely a failure to have the patience to take the time necessary to really look over and evaluate the complex situations modern society presents hand over fist. The human brain we are given can do this. It can find the twists, the flaws, and the dangers in our plans and our thinking. You simply have to learn to spend the right amounts of time thinking, at the right times. Once you do, your native intelligence can work at its best. Gradually, rational processes of mind will become second nature.

The two foundations of rational thought and behavior are logic and process.

The root meaning of the word, "logic", comes from the Greek word, "Logos". Logos refers to the true interconnectedness of all known and unknown worldly phenomena, all intertwined in a deep web of cause and effect, all things related in some way, each affecting the other. When we are logical, we are usually acting and deciding from a very good understanding of how the real world really works, and the ways that it can become. Being logical is simply exercising a keenly intelligent realism, and being guided by its understandings. The proving ground of rationality is in application. We apply, like a tool, our understandings of reality in our actions to make a better world, for ourselves, kith and kin, one hopes, and if we are rational, this works out more often than not.

This inner logos that forms as we become more rational in the progressions of our thought and behavior arises from the simple processes of animal intelligence. We observe the consequences to our thoughts and actions, good or bad. We see what works and what does not work. Things that are beneficial, we learn to do better. Things that bring harm, we learn to avoid. Either our inner understandings of the world are true and work in favor of our existence in positive ways, or they are in error, and lead us into mistakes, problems, and wasted efforts. The process of intelligence operates throughout this experience of actual results, and if we are concerned about such things, begins to identify those patterns of conscious phenomena that keep producing sensible results for us. Learning from our mistakes is the most natural thing we do.

Ironically, human rationality is the only rationality in the animal kingdom that is ever at risk. Except in the degenerations of age or disease, you will never find a lower animal behave in any way other than what is rational for it to do given its circumstances and nature. The animal's brain limits what it can perceive as relevant stimuli in its environment, and its behavioral responses are quite spare, but what an animal does, when compared to what it comprehends its situation to be, invariably makes good, common sense, even if it does not work. The prospects of a rhino charging a big game hunter are not good, but its response to the perception of real danger is appropriate, and the best a rhino can do.

Thanks to the fabulous stretches of the human cerebral cortex, our rational behavior comes off looking a great deal smarter than that of the animals. But this same biological equipment holds the seeds of perplexion. We can engage in and get hooked on patterns in conscious experience that have no rational sense at all. We will form opinions on unevaluated rumors and stereotypes. We develop close ended attitudes with their no brainer, knee jerk responses. More disturbingly, the human psyche lies exposed to the malformations of the Freudian Underground, where inner conflicts, fixations, indulgent immaturities, self delusions, and self serving rationalizations, dumb down our behavior. Only humans manage to be mean, ugly, and stupid in the face of a given potential to be generous, pleasant and noble.

Perhaps the most compelling evidence that human rationality is at risk is that we all seem especially pleased to be able to identify something as a matter of common sense, as pleased as we would be to have seen a falling star. If it were not rare, the act of pointing out common sense with pride would seem mundane and unremarkable. Were we invested in the same primal rationality of the lower animals, we would not need a word for rational behavior.

The Weed Garden

The primal rationality the lower animals enjoy follows from simple natural selection. Stupid, irrational behaviors weed themselves out of the gene pool, or the species dies out. Animals operate at the limit of their evolved biological package. There is no more envelope to push. Try teaching a cow how to become a better cow.

In contrast, the human biological package, when it appeared, was an advance far beyond its evolutionary context. From our first signs 100,000 years ago in the highlands of East Africa to our appearance in Europe, the Middle East, and the Mediterranean 65,000 years later, the selective advantage of the species, the rational processes these new brains carried, never leveled off. We became such proficient hunters and gatherers that we hunted and gathered ourselves into scarce game and poor pickings. But over a couple of millennia, we figured out agriculture and reset the "population to food supply" equation so much in our favor that we could afford civilization and this modern society that has followed so far. We not only adapt to the strange new conditions of civilization, we cause its ways to progress even more, bringing about even newer conditions no human has ever lived in before, let alone have had time to adapt to biologically.

Humans seem to have no end of envelope to push on. The limits to our evolutionary advances are still very uncertain. We go from the telegraph to the internet in a hundred years. We dream in THX special effects, and through our works of science fiction, journey to the stars and back.

The driving cause behind all this material and civilized progress is the last set of biological changes to occur in the human genus, the enlarged frontal lobe with its capacity for mediating conscious thought, and our highly developed capacity for language. Humans experience a daunting array of conscious phenomena, most often in linguistic or visual modalities. These conscious events can transpire at fantastic rates, and are often far removed and unrelated to the stimulus and response environment of the immediate animal present. Some of these progressions of mediating conscious experience work for us, some work against us, and many are just inconsequential.

But individual mental prowess was not all we got in this last burst of evolution. When we have a good idea, we can talk about it. If one does not know, another might, then all know.

Through language, we can share plans, solve common problems, coordinate actions, and pass on a cultural heritage to a next generation. Between language, our cooperative genius, and our bigger brain, humans have had a distinctly unfair advantage over the rest of the animal kingdom, and have cheated the forces of history and nature several times in the past to get this far, this modern society we all count so much upon.

The range and virtuosity of human conscious life is impressive, but it comes without an instruction manual. You have to write your own. Some patterns and progressions in conscious experience are productive, some are incidental or dysfunctional. Some uplift us while others drag us down. Some strengthen us while others twist us up into miscreant and malformed beings. This is the weed garden. It contains weeds and flowers. The human mind must be cultivated to fulfill its promise. You must find the weeds of your conscious life and root them out. Where you find a flower, nurture it. The stakes are simple. Does your mind serve you, as it was evolved to do, or do you dangle at the ends of the strings it pulls.

There seems to be nothing humans can't think or feel if we provoke ourselves. We will think hundreds of thoughts an hour when we have a lot to think about, and think hundreds of thoughts when we do not. The mind, in its effort to serve our purposes and attend to our needs, as if in celebration of its sheer capacity, can bring up all manner of conscious events, some irrelevant, some silly, some mean, some pointed, and many self gratifying. Not nearly everything we think needs to be thought. Since this conscious life is private, unless we personally identify the immaterial and the self indulgent, and set about weeding them out from the stream of consciousness we experience as ourselves, the unproductive, dysfunctional progressions of thought and feeling will grow as readily as the constructive progressions of rational thought and feeling. The weeds flourish with the flowers, but only for a while. Unless you learn to cultivate your mind, your conscious life will finally overgrow with weeds.

The cultivation of mind is essentially a problem of learning how to enforce selection on your conscious experience. We can identify what grinds our teeth or wastes our emotion on bitter dregs. We can see what is unbecoming, negative, or unworthy, and determine to rend these kinds of mental events from our future stream of consciousness, even if one has to root them out everyday for half a lifetime. This is the life of self examination at work, not just to see and know what you would have done differently, but to change, and in fact, do differently, in mind, in feeling, and in conduct, next time around.

The same evolutionary serendipity that confronts us with the weed garden challenge, this problem of selectively shaping our conscious experience, provides us with a tool to work with. The human brain can not only closely follow the progressions of its own inner mediational behavior, it can remember and review those progressions in mind, along with the circumstances occurring simultaneously in the external environment, with almost the same intensity as the first time around, sometimes noticing relevant facts not noticed when the experience was actually taking place.

Humans are capable of thinking about their thinking. Our mind's eye sees what we are and what we can be, and our spirit wills the change. This is a long, uncompromising struggle, but gradually, through belief that change is possible, and a steady, refocusing effort, we can win positives changes, and lose the useless, the wasted, and the irrational aspects of our mental lives.

Look upon your conscious experience of this human existence, every minute of it, as a precious gift not to be ruined. For every negative or self indulgent episode of conscious experience, ask yourself, what else could I be feeling? Certainly life brings pains, hurts, shocks, discouragements, and other bad happenings. To find that you experience angers, envies, selfish wants, and the like, is to know yourself as human. You will make natural human responses. But leave the negative ones in the rivers of the past. Weed them out, and let your natural intelligence lead you to the patterns and processes of rational behavior.

With the same determination of purpose, strengthen the good patterns and progressions. There are many good things that the human can experience in inner consciousness, and many good ways of thinking. External aids and guides can help, but you do not have to rely on them. You are as apt to experience positive and renewing progressions of inner life as you are negative ones. The good thinking patterns will be there for you to see. Mark them and reinforce them. They will internalize and come back. This is what makes within the free thinker a sure inner character that sensibly guides and shapes one's processes of mind. Even under duress, a free thinker will generate rational and positive progressions of independently motivated conscious experience. Learn to nurture the ways of mind that are good for you. Finish with a garden full of flowers in bloom, instead of choking weeds.

Some Useful Rational Processes

There are far more good and bad habits of mind than any brief manual can cover and still be brief. What is offered here is a workable core set of objects, which if reached and strengthened, will work to push out the inferior patterns of your conscious life. Find the others on your own and name them in your own way. The useful progressions you can train into your thinking should number no less than the tools one might find in a dog soldier's garage.

Concentration

Concentration is the focusing of all one's conscious energy and mental ability on one thing, and then holding it on that one thing for serious lengths of time. The opposite of a mind that can concentrate as needed is the haphazard, shallow, scatter brained, distracted mind. This capacity to focus, to concentrate with singular determination, comes from the evolved predator nature in the human species. The requirements of the hunt are a severe selective force. The predator must seek, track, and lock in upon its prey. Then, through a combination of tactics, attack and bring it down. As the prey animal has itself evolved to evade and escape predations, the distracted hunter starves.

Some segments of modern society lament and confess shame that the human seems such a highly evolved killer when the need becomes extreme. This is juvenile foolishness. All the abilities that make up the human difference can be employed poorly or well, to good effect or for evil. The problem is not in the ability to hunt and kill, or in any of the other two sided abilities. We have found many other ways to feed ourselves and get along with each other. The decisive factor lies in the will of the spirit. Can it take control of its own shaping, or is it mercilessly shaped by any and all that breaking reality throws at it?

The general effect of concentration and focus, this centering of heart and mind, is to bring an undivided being to the moment of action, where intuitive play is unleashed onto breaking events, all primed for the spontaneous adjustments that play will require as the play unfolds. This focused presence can be seen in the pronounced mental set both athletes and soldiers show in the moments just before kickoff or mission jump off. Mind, body, and soul are focused as one in one downbeat, one breath, as the moment of action approaches. Fail in concentration, and many things do not get done, some go wrong, and everything else takes longer.

Emotional intensity is often mistaken for concentration, but is something different. Many times emotional intensity is actually an obstacle to effective thinking and action. Yet at other times, we deliberately seek the combination of concentration and emotive intensity. Resonance in heart, mind and body, heightens performance, whether on the playing fields, or in the streets, or the lurking wilds of the real world.

Yet to be concentrated, all you have to do is keep your mind on what it is doing when it is doing it. You can concentrate in a peaceful, emotional calm, just as readily as you can fire yourself up. What you want are intelligent, creative emotional currents underwriting your moves, not some overbearing sense of yourself and your presumed abilities.

Noticing

A good habit of mind to develop is that of noticing things, the patterns in events and circumstances, and the relationships between them, whether they be features of the environment, the behaviors of others and oneself, the workings of your mind, or the interplay between them. Pay attention to detail and you will find that the details take care of you, either in spotting trouble or possibility, or in preventing hosts of petty problems and hassles.

Every setting, situation, or ground you may find yourself in, be it a bus stop, a bank lobby, or some dentist's office, contains the imprints and traces of past events, the obvious present, and the indications of future happenings. Noticing is the basis for the tracking skill of the hunter, to see and study the signs, knowing their causes and their implications. Such knowledge is often instrumental in accomplishing the pursuits we undertake.

Aggressive paying attention is essentially the animal's natural orientation response to the conditions and moving events happening in its immediate environment. We perceive and interpret, and combine all we observe in the present, intuitive moment, what some call court sense, or field sense, or even street sense.

Learn to look to the four directions where ever you are. Study them and your immediate environment. This is where you are. Will you need a photograph to know you were there?

What one wants is an observing, thinking mind, the Sherlock Holmes mind, one given to observation and studied deduction. This is our primary way of knowing things, for it is personal, flowing from our experience, and not from what others say or think, whether in books, television chatter, or oral hearsay. In those cases of second hand knowledge, we depend on the soundness and truthfulness of someone else's mind. When you can see and judge for yourself, accept no second hand alternative.

Facility and Flexibility

You want your mind to be capable of many things, and you want it to be able to move easily from one thing to another as needed, finding efficiency and effectiveness in attending to the purposes you set for yourself.

A mind possessing facility will have acquired and developed many diverse skills to apply in handling situations and problems as they arise in daily, real life. It will be knowledgeable and quick to identify the relevance of that knowledge and how it applies to present matters. It will be able to evaluate, judge, consider, size up and check out, compare, plan, interpret, imagine, and carry out logical procedures and empirical methods.

Flexibility is the ability of the mind to move decisively from present thought processes to new and different ones, or back to important earlier

ones, as new situations, events, or information warrant. A fixated mind
that cannot let go of a particular idea or pattern of thought is usually ineffective in solving problems, and especially ineffective in dealing with the
complex, fast breaking situations of reality. You want the progressions of
your thinking to range freely over your inner landscape instead burrowing
in a rabbit hole and hibernating.

Strategic and Tactical Thinking

We have many drives and motives, some of which are necessary to
physical existence, some which pertain to social relations, and some which
we personally set for ourselves. Human life is doing. We are given the
human mind to make that doing go well.

The business of accomplishment is the province of strategy and tactics,
the why's, wherefore's, and the how to's of achieving ends and getting
things done. Look to employ all your resources, what you have available as
material means and what you have available as mental abilities, when you
set accomplishment before yourself. Study the outcomes of your purposes
and efforts against your original plans and assessments. The goal is to get
done well what you plan to do, and do so decisively and with dispatch.

The first guideline of strategy and tactics is to think first in term of
objectives and why they matter. Then allow your mind to explore the logic
of implications and means freely. Set your sights, then go to work. Keep
your eye on the objective.

The second guideline is play the field as you find it. Be realistic and empirical. Strategy and tactics only work when they have a foundation in truth.

The third guideline is to make the moves your current positions
affords. Do what you can, now.

But the prime directive of strategy and tactics is to start. Move, learn,
imagine, and move again. The process will work for you, but only if you
get underway.

As you pursue goals, see and know what is going on around you. Know the tracks and traces of past happenings. Watch the breaking realities of the present moment. See the applications to your strategic and tactical thinking. See the constraints and the opportunities. Be patient or aggressive enough to make good moves.

Try not to prejudice the future. This usually limits the real future. We can befuddle ourselves with box canyon mirages, and see only reason after reason why something cannot be done. This may be impressive analysis, but it is not strategy. Strategy engages the future by beginning it.

Review and Reflection

We are capable of playing back in our minds the stream of events once occurring in past situations, conversations, and our participations in them, as if all were on videotape. Sometimes we notice things in our reflections that we missed when we were experiencing matters directly.

From such inner review, we can make judgements. We can see mistakes, bad moves and good moves, in ourselves and in others. We can approve or disapprove our actions. We can like what we see, or feel shame and guilt.

The first payoffs of these reflective processes of mind are practical. We can keep on thinking about a problem, a plan, or a situation, some puzzle we need to work out, and sometimes we do finally figure it out right. Much of apparently ordinary thinking is habitual review and reflection bringing back ideas, issues, purposes, and the like, to immediate consciousness for further working over. We get smarter because we think things out.

But review and reflection also make the moral sense possible. These are the tools of self betterment. We can see our past actions and their context in our mind's eye, and see the consequences they provoked, whether for good or for bad. We can take the time tosee more deeply into our lives and our actions. Did our actions hurt others, or boost them? Did they cheat virtue, or honor it? Did you feel good about the result, or poorly? We can judge and learn things by our thinking and want to do better. We can see the better sides of ourselves, and the less impressive. We can chart a better course for our future conduct to take on, and even realize inner changes that make that better way a reality. But only provided we have the willpower to change our act to fit the virtues and ideals we hold for ourselves.

Rhythm

We live in real time and space, which means that there are many events happening around us, and within us, all simultaneously and one after another. Rhythm is there whether we find it or not. Getting the natural rhythms to work for us makes mental and emotional life more sustainable and stable. Creating rhythm in our endeavors, be they mundane or profound, speeds attainment, carries motivation forward, and even makes the apparent drudgery more endurable, even enjoyable. Ask any track laying railroad crew.

The object is to see and feel the rhythms and cadences in the simultaneous flows of the many events occurring in conscious experience, between thought, feeling, and the animal's business, that continuous flow of our own behavior within the myriad of external scenes and sequences that make up the environment we must live in, this real world. The skill is acquired when we learn how to catch good rhythms when they happen, to change rhythms when the rhythms change, and to recover rhythm when it falls apart. We learn the dance of doing, living, being. A rhythmic mind is not only more productive, it is also more emotionally pleased. If you do not find yourself breaking into a hum or a tune from time to time, the rhythms of your life are probably being more done unto you than done by you.

Peace

The natural mind is at bottom a peaceful mind. Occasions for furious thought and a fired up heart will happen, sometimes in rapid successions. But the natural mind moves into and out of these from a background sense of calm, peace, and satisfaction. Peace is the basis and baseline of balance.

In the long run, this underwriting peacefulness comes partly from learning how to control your thinking, stopping its knack for constant, often feverish, thought that gets one nowhere. But one also must learn how to cultivate and practice those things that bring us emotional satisfaction, creating peace within ourselves, as reliably as we might make a meal, or take a hot bath, clean and refresh ourselves.

Residing in extended moments of pure consciousness, being simply aware and breathing, but without chatter of thought, sets the deeper currents of emotional being in motion. Quick and alive, pure consciousness rests and renews the brain in all its charges, mental, emotional, and physical. Whether you understand such behavior as prayer or meditation, learn to bring this boon into your conscious experience every day, just as you would take a long drink of life giving water.

For the monk, inner calm, once found, becomes easier and easier to dwell in, for there is little real world reality breaking about their seclusion to disrupt it. The dog soldier's lot is not so simple. Inner calm is a daily objective. To live and strive in the real world often means shooting its rapids and breakers, day in and day out. The impress of intensity, purpose, and the impinging environment, leaves us wound up, and naturally so.

The dog soldier must learn the art of unwinding. Find the time and the spaces for those patterns of behavior that rachet you down. Whether through self pampering, listening to music, hand crafts, or leisurely walks, allow the urgent intentions, past and present, to arise and beg attention in new, wide open spaces of consciousness. They fly up like erratic, leaking balloons, and are released, one after another, from their pressing duty, each now at ease and on standby. As intentions let go, direct the flow of the emotional energy leaning on each into the body like a ground wire. The tight, emotional set that comes from driving the reckless streets of civilized life gradually drains away, and the inner calm returns and stays.

The Simple Starting Position

All these rational processes are just ways of lining up your thinking, those progressions of conscious phenomena of this sort or that. So just work on your thinking as you would your body's physical prowess. Use and experience, combined with native intelligence, improves most things.

Pay attention to your thought, its processes and patterns. Know them. Identify them. Judge them. And then modify and guide your thinking accordingly. Learn how not to think when your brain needs rest.

Make time for thinking, not by schedule but by need. Get your thinking time in every day, wherever you have space and time to do it.

Finally, feed your thinking time. Read and take control of your own education. Learn through books, videos, and literature the many things of the world, its history, ideas, and sciences, its peoples and their ways, and above all, learn about the human being that you are. Observe, and consider. Ponder notions or ideas, ones you've heard and ones of your own making. Study and perfect your expressions of the meanings that occur within your mind. Work at finding the right words, the right phrases and metaphors that communicate what you really mean, the worthwhile understanding that you have found.

Learn all the good things that thinking is good for, and lose the habits of mind that are useless, babbling, vain, and anxiety producing. Just like you tend a garden, cultivating the flowers and pulling out the weeds. Think in silence as well as in thought.

Above all, look forward. What life you have had is behind. You have had it. The life you have left is before you, ahead. Look forward to living it. Think about it. Envision it. Understand that no plan ever survives contact with reality intact. Expect change, and expect yourself to know when to change. Improvise at will. Life can be very entertaining and gratifying when you are participating and growing with it.

Emotionality

Your emotionality is real life happening to you now. It is your primary conscious experience of this human existence each of us must know and live. We remember how we felt during a significant experience with far more aclarity and sureness than we remember what we were thinking at the time. You can banish a thought, but try feeling nothing without feeling something, even if indescribable.

As if plagued by biblical curses, for most of the three thousand years of so called Western civilization, emotions have been demonized. Our natural, direct relationship to our emotionality has been fractured and fragmented, and generally screwed up. The first curse was delivered by Aristotle, who divided human experience into mind body dualism. The mind, possessed of the soul, was perfect and of another world. The body was everything imperfect, corruptible, and perishable. The Greeks saw, as we still see today, that strong emotions are a powerful force in human conduct, sometimes leading to dramatically unpleasant ends. In anger, a man kills his brother, then regrets the deed. Easy to blame emotionality for the evil. The fact that humans also coldly reason out plans that end in disaster somehow escaped Aristotle's notice.

The second curse is religion's recent insistence upon universal original sin. Emotions are again consigned to the body, and chained to the equation, flesh equals temptation, equals evil, equals damnation. If you smile, you might risk your soul. Strong emotions must certainly will. Puritans typically have poor emotional control once they have any. So contrived are their ways, that they have no experience with natural life emotionality at all.

The truth is that emotionality is a brain centered process, arising in the basal ganglia in the very heart of the brain. Emotions themselves are conscious experiences that are as genuinely "mental" as thought. Like all natural capacities, sometimes they work with us. Sometimes they work against us. The challenge is to understand their ways and then to cull them. Even animals recognize this and learn self control as they mature.

But most of the emotional life of the animal is direct, that is, it sensibly fits what is going on in the immediate environment. Even the dog that whimpers sadly on his master's grave is fitting the emotional response to the present reality. Humans also have this direct and natural emotional rhythm with present reality. But because we are capable of vast quantities of mediational conscious phenomena, we can also induce emotions indirectly. We can be riding on a bus, see our mother's grave in our consciousness, and feel sad enough to leak tears. In fact, humans are capable of experiencing most of their emotional life through progressions of thought and induced emotions. We can live in our minds.

Like most natural capacities, these mediational progressions mixing thought and induced emotion can work for us, and against us. For example, you might take on the tasks and chores of planning and preparing for the 50th anniversary of your mother and father. As you do this work, you might think of the many good moments together, and how proud they were, and feel lots of little good feelings. By the actual event, you would be awash in swelling currents of positive emotion.

But in the same way, repetitive progressions of thought can become linked to negative emotions. Human can nurse angers, bear grudges, feed envy, and wallow in self pity or delusion. These fixations of mind are the stuff of the Freudian Underground, dysfunctional and self defeating. When negative emotions become drivers of self feeding cycles of thought and feeling, bad things tend to happen, inside and out. You forget happiness, lose friends, and alienate strangers. Eventually your body caves in to the unfair psychosomatic flogging, and gets sick in some way. Negative progressions ruin conscious experience and wreck the body, finally ruining life itself.

Study your emotional landscape. Look for these unique creatures of human conscious experience, these tight, recurrent progressions that feed emotion off thought, and thought back off emotion. Do they do you any good, or do they waste your precious conscious life? Do they leave you in the breezes of finer emotional feeling, or do they leave you grinding your teeth or rubbing your brow?

Emotional life is wonderful stuff. All satisfaction, contentment, and happiness is emotional. When it is time to be peaceful, you should be able to feel peaceful and satisfied. When it is time to perform, you should be able to stir up enthusiasm that rides well with accomplishment.

You will have good emotions and bad, and many shades in between. Learn the rhythm and flows of emotionality. Know and reinforce the good ones. Emotional life can become a long running dance you can guide and anticipate. Unknown yet rich emotional experiences lie before all of us. But the best are only attainable after learning, and appreciating over many years, all the melodies, motifs, and crescendos possible in an original human life.

Emotional Conditioning

The goal of emotional conditioning is to influence and shape the emotional progressions in your conscious experience as one might influence and shape the flows of rain down a watershed's landscape, ready to catch the deluges bound to occur, and ready to channel it all toward constructive ends. Because emotions are our primary conscious experience, and are as ever present as our breathing, emotions must be conditioned directly. With physical or mental conditioning, you can practice or exercise aspects of the forms in which you plan to perform. You can develop the skill. It makes no sense to work emotions this way. You cannot practice or prepare for feeling good, you just feel good or not. There is no skill involved.

But the lack of a practice effect does not mean you cannot learn to understand and deal with your emotional currents.

The general object is to focus your awareness on your emotional life, and observe and be cognizant of its features and provocations, that is, give emotional experiences their due recognition. Accept them as they happen, see why they happen, then let them play out under your will. None last all that long unless you nurse them. You will learn your susceptibilities and how to brace for them. You will discover the ways that handle the strong emotions and channel them. You will see how to encourage and enjoy your emotional life, and feel better and more fulfilled for the experience.

Emotionality presents us with the same weed garden problem that confronts us when we look over our thinking. Not all emotional progressions we have work for us or lead to a better quality of living. Strong emotions can be a great strength in the human, but the ancients were correct in observing that when we fail to channel them well, bad things, like social chaos and personal disaster, tend to happen. Then there are the straight out negative emotions, fear, hatred, self pity, vengefulness, envy, and so on. These are like blights and plagues upon our conscious experience. Even many positive emotions are not especially worthwhile. Emotions like selfishness, vanity, self righteousness, and presumed superiority, are irrational and anti-social. They seldom make for a positive inner life over the long run.

The first object of emotional conditioning is to recognize and accept that all emotional response is natural. We are not evil just because we get mad enough inside to want to hit someone for their injustice to others. So when an emotion comes on strong and negative, recognize that it is a genuine response to your current situation, even if you'd rather it weren't. Don't fight the emotion. Ride it. Self control is largely a measure of accepting the emotion in its time, walking her home, then returning to rational processes.

The second object of emotional conditioning is to weigh your emotional episodes, looking for their true effects on you. Apply the simple economic equation of opportunity costs. What benefit did you really get from the episode, at what cost, compared to what you might have otherwise experienced emotionally? If you spend hours brooding in rancor, or pimping your self esteem, what did it get you? Were you somehow incapable of doing something more worthwhile with your emotional life? Find these weeds and mark them for extinction. Don't thumbsuck your emotional life away.

The third object of emotional conditioning is to fight down negative emotions. If possible, drown them in positive ones. In addition to the simple insistence of will power, use your processes of thought to quell, instead of encourage, the misguided emotion. You can train your mind to its own command vocabulary. You can set the intentions centers of the brain to reject the negative emotion when it appears, and if your minds panders to it, to stomp on the process. If the negative emotion is induced, tell your mind to stop inducing it, and induce something else. It takes a little bit longer than a smart dog would need to learn and respond to such commands of inner mind, but it happens. You can tell your mind to be silent. You can command your feeling to be done with. Both delivered with an emotional punch in their own right. Then you move on to better subjects of conscious experience.

Do not expect dramatic changes. There is no one drenching emotional experience, or sudden insight of wisdom, that will wholly transform your inner life overnight. But the same power that can trap us in the Freudian Underground, can work to shape the inner landscapes upon which the rivers of emotionality flow. We find the ways that better suit our better sense of self. This is the river and land approach to emotional control. You cannot tell the river not to flow, but you can shape its courses over time, and channels its currents to better effect. Sometimes you even have moments where you call the dance and your emotions answer in harmony.

The fourth object of emotional conditioning is to find and cultivate the flowers of emotional experience with the same thoroughness you root out the weeds. What are the conditions that bring about pleasing feelings and good moods? What progressions of thought and induced emotion uplift us or nurture us? Which renew and rejuvenate? Can you smell the roses?

Human existence can find more than enough suffering and misery from fortune alone. Self inflicted misery is senseless and irrational. There are simply too many positive and good emotional experiences available. We can be peaceful, serene, interested, amused, curious, delighted, adventuresome, satisfied, and full of good humor, happily present and ready to enjoy, if given any chance at all. These are the mediational progressions of conscious experience you want, where the mixture of thought and feeling flow into and build upon one another until a stubborn positive nature dominates your emotionality. There are too many good and fine moods possible in the human to waste any precious lifetime on the misbegotten and the malformed.

Above all, learn what moves your emotions. As a natural capacity, the induction of good emotional states is satisfying and self reinforcing. We love, even crave, having our emotions stirred and deeply moved, whether in aesthetic appreciations or in meaningful deeds. Eventually, the everyday events of life can become moving.

The final object is to internalize the dynamic of good humor to the extent that it is with you always and ready to play. If your emotional life is not fun anymore, you had better make some changes before it is too late. Losing the ability to play, to have fun, and to find good humor in unusual circumstances, alone or with others, is like breathing air without oxygen, only you just die inside. You still have to live the rest of your natural life, what natural is left of it.

Expressive Behavior

In the end, learning some body of words on how to live, and taking the prescribed actions in accordance with the programs of discipline they propose, is relatively easy. Eventually you have to just live, in the present, one scene after another. If your code and your discipline to not show up in your regular living, the whole enterprise is vain. The point is to really be changing for the better, and to see this awakening expressed in every scene that finds its way into the rivers of your life.

You cannot lead a life of virtue missing its many ordinary occasions. Most times we just live, with no great deeds apparent, no great stakes on the table, no defining moment at hand. In fact, most of human life is simply animal living with no great issues in the balance. The Heroic, the Tragic, and the Romantic are great moments, but we spend most of our lives in between these times. You cannot wait for life to lend you its great moments. We are alive in all moments, conscious, thoughtful, sentient, and corporeal. As living is an expression of the spirit, so all our behavior, moment to moment, is an expression of our original character. Missing the opportunities of personal expression is like missing part of your life.

All the facets of conscious being, the mental, the emotional, and the physical, combine simultaneously in the animal present of personal expression. The object is to find in every venue its potential for an original expression of the presence of our inner character. Better, to make that expression directly and intuitively.

Some unfortunate trends in twentieth century masculine emasculation have made too many men, both old and young, stiff, uptight, goofy, repressive, or ineffectual. The Puritan approach to manhood actually amounts to castration. The body is dull and dully dressed, but cinched up tight. The face is pale, unseeing, and acutely self conscious. These men are dead on the outside, even if true masculine qualities endure on the inside.

From this sad reality has come the specious complaint by women that men are not in touch with their emotions. In truth, a man can no more be out of touch with his emotions than can a woman. But modern men face far more arbitrary sanctions on their expressive behavior, and often end up stylizing some oddly acceptable form of mental and emotional constipation at an early age. The human male makes a miserable herd animal. No dog soldier would accept such a fate.

Expressive behavior in the human is as natural to the male as to the female, even if the manner and occasions of expression differ somewhat. We often find expressive behavior pleasing in its own right, and as we mature in character, it becomes confirmational. It is who we are and what we worked to become, original, understandable, fully present, keenly involved, and expressing the differences unique to our personal way, through word, or gesture, or maybe only be silent look.

The human animal has gifts of natural expressiveness that are without parallel in the animal kingdom. Wolves and dogs can howl at the moon, but the human can sing a thousand songs in a thousand voices. We respond to the rhythm of music, and dance, in a thousand different ways, for no earthly purpose other than when we dance well, it works wonderful physical and emotional effects upon us.

Most animals play when young, and show curiosity and a knack for discovery. But they are soon adult animals and the survival pattern of the animal life of dull routines dominates them. Humans stay curious, play freely, and seek and enjoy discovery all through life. Engaging in these behaviors expresses our unique human nature. When we fulfill that nature, we experience a little more enjoyment in living, and little more confirmation of our original identity. In a word, we feel a real human being and it feels good.

There are no special objects for expressive behavior except to engage in it, master your ways of doing it, and accept no final discouragements. These are perhaps the most interesting choices of your life, for they define you in the present, real world, whether in public or in private. Life without expression is mere existence.

Answer to all the seasons of expressive behavior. Sing when the song is in your heart. Dance when the rhythm moves you. Play when the fun is there to have. Sometimes we express our being in alertness and private understanding. Sometimes there is a game face to put on. At other times, mirth and gaiety to enjoy. How often do you smile to yourself, or even chuckle? Laugh, be serious, grieve, and exalt, all when their time arrives. These are the times of your life. Do you want to miss them? If you are uptight and constipated, you will.

Spirituality

Seek. Save for a few philosophic cults scattered throughout history, all human cultures have held one belief in common, that of a crossover, of the survival of a personal spirit beyond the sure, physical death in this world.

Fast, meditate, pray, and ponder. All methods may aid in the quest. All methods may fail as well. So rely first on what you can see with eyes and brains you seem to have as gift, that consciousness and intelligence that make who you are without your having had anything to do with the matter. Observe the wonders of the universe, the miracle of life and the finality of death. Then wonder at the greatest miracle of all, that you exist with brain enough to witness these things, and glimpse, maybe even grasp for just a moment, all that is more.

It is said that there are no atheists in foxholes. It might be equally true that there are no atheists on the frontier. They have either died off, vanished without a trace, or gone home. There has never been a tribal culture without strong, emotionally driven, spiritual practices and beliefs. Offerings, invocations, ceremonies, sacrifices, and celebrations dominate primitive tribal life. These practices, their verbal orchestrations, and their emblematic relics, often find special focus in the warrior's life. The vagaries and happenstance of combat are too great, too obvious, for even the most skilled warrior to settle for a merely intellectualized spiritual understanding.

Indeed, personal spiritual integrity, with the beliefs and the guides to conduct that come with this condition, was regarded as the Cheyenne warrior's most essential weapon. The medicine of kindred animal spirits, the sacred totems and tokens, spawn courage and great deeds, and prepare and ready the warrior for the face of death, willingly accepted in defense of the people.

The American Plains Indian saw the attainment of spiritual grace as an individual endeavor. You cannot find God for some one else. They must find such foundations alone, and in their own way, as it comes to them. The vision quest set before older boys ready for passage into manhood sought to provide each individual with their own guides and keys, their own personal medicine. The theologies which framed the personal quest were simple and uncontentious. There was little possibility of heresy or blasphemy. No need for crosses, stakes, or faggots.

Another instructive tribal approach to individual spirituality is found among the Australian Aborigines. These people are the oldest, enduring culture on record, isolated on the island continent and its vast desolations known as the Outback for over ten thousand years. When a certain kind of yearning came upon a man, it was expected that he would go out on a walkabout, perhaps for several years, wandering whither the will and intuition led him, anywhere and all over the wilderness Outback, searching for the experiences that the yearnings had called for.

For their bearings, the Australian Aborigine sought out the dreamsongs of the land as it lay before them. In the purifications of solitude and self reliance, the wanderer opened their consciousness to the intimations of another, spiritual, reality, laying over the terrain like a second landscape. As the dreamsong called, the seeker moved, like a hunter on an unseen trail. You stayed out on the walkabout until the yearnings that had first moved you were fulfilled. Then you headed home.

Unfortunately, most "civilized" religions are theologically complex beyond comprehension. Too much store is set upon articulating truth in words in order to define one religion in contradistinction to dozens of other religions using different words and phrasings. When the difference is then thought to insure one's salvation and righteousness against the fate of mistaken fools and false prophets, religion ends up cursed with the European Social Disease. If you believe that your religion and its profession by you, makes you better than others, setting you above them, as more favored in God's Eyes, then you may be the model of piety, but you have failed the spiritual test of kinship.

Human life should be an ongoing spiritual process, a continuing quest to deepen spiritual understanding. There are many "how to" forms, techniques, and programs to be found among the many human cultures and their religions. For the Cheyenne and other Plains Indians, the vision quest and the sun dance stand out, but nearly everything they did beckoned to the greater insight. Spiritual moments could come at anytime. If you were Cheyenne, you were watching for them all the time.

"Civilized" programs of organized religion are usually not nearly so demanding. You go through relatively simple rites, memorize and recite by rote a specific creed and its wordings, practice by attending church meetings, and you are good to go. As advertised, salvation is easy. Much easier than losing weight or quitting smoking.

Do not fool yourself, or be overconfident. Developing a genuine spiritual sense in the human is the most difficult of human undertakings. Be skeptical of short cuts.

Human spirituality drives human growth and the readiness for that growth, and in return, the spirit is strengthened and deepened by such growth. If there truly be a human spirit fit to make the unknown crossover, it will possess the same fires that burn in this life. As we grow, the spirit must grow, for we are the same. As we possess a potential to fulfill, so possesses the spirit a potential it must fulfill. Human life is not some shell to be husked. It is, rather, a nurturing womb from which we are born into the next world.

What we do in this life matters, for what we do, save manna from heaven, is the only food our soul will have to grow upon. That is what the moral life is, a good feeding of the spirit and the inner growth it causes. Be moral first, and when spirituality comes to you, you will find that it was there all along.

The only object for spirituality in the dog soldier discipline is to engage yourself. See what it is all about for your self. Look upon your life as a journey of many spiritual quests, happenings, and defining moments. As you allow such intuitions and intimations to lead you, you will create within yourself the experiences from which all spiritual things grow. Keep it simple. Follow the light and stay away from the darkness.

True spiritual understanding brings emotional satisfaction and emotional strength. It is the peace that passes understanding. It is the grace to endure. It is the position of the Manual that the dog soldier find spirituality for themselves, by whatever paths, rites and rituals, tried, embraced or abandoned. And when the seeds of a greater mind blossom, when the roots grow deep inside you, your spirituality will become terribly personal and as original as you are. It will be something no one can take from you. But you are now likely to fail the many tests of conformity that organized religions require of the pure and the orthodox. But that will not matter. You will know. What is between Man and God belongs there, between Man and God.

If you cannot apprehend God directly, no faith in words
can ever make up the difference.

Personal Presence

The combination of corporal, thoughtful, emotional, and spiritual being, united in the present moment of animal existence, is what we call personal presence. You want to live in the present with significant presence, a complete presence, one composed of presence of mind, presence of feeling, presence of person, presence of purpose, and presence of spirit. Learn to find and lock into this consciousness everywhere you are. Sit by yourself in a corner, or wander a shopping mall crowd at Christmas, everywhere you are, you will find this united presence happening in you if you evoke it. There is no virtual human existence. You have to be present through every second of it. Can you find the simple present? The sage motto that advises us to live in the present really first implies that we can find it. Can you collapse the past and the encroaching future, and just be where you currently exist, just for now, all dimensions of being in rhythm and focused, ready to invest reality as it breaks around you?

Do not let your mind become plagued with too many visitations from the past, especially when the lessons to learn were logged in long ago. Neither let your mind overplan and worry too much about the future. It will come. Be confident you can face it squarely because you have kept yourself ready. Know that you will learn from it in any event. Confidence takes the fall in stride with the gain.

Feel the inner expanse and nature of your present physical state, your posture and animal purpose. Measure the depth of your breathing, and your ever ready awareness of what is happening now. Allow your emotional consciousness to flow like a swift, deep river, and understand that when you are shooting rapids, it will feel like shooting rapids. When you slip onto the slow, mile wide rivers, it will feel like the lazy Mississippi. When you live in the present, you become instinctively open to its possibilities, where each spontaneous act you make makes you more original. Freedom creates.

If you concede that there is a next world you will be born into, how you live this human life will have a lot to do with how that goes. You want to be fully present as it happens, and through your presence, involved. Creation has only begun. Stay with it.

Animal Matters

Part of the lore of dog soldier ways is to recover the natural animal sense as to what is good for the animalness and what is bad for the animalness, and to be able to act and behave accordingly without suffering the oddish feelings that civilized mien and mores produce to reinforce their artificiality. Our animal nature should be a source of strength not an embarrassment.

Our animalness needs to be tended, just as our uniquely human aspects need cultivation. When we treat the animal like a push button soft machine, or some disagreeable tumor unfortunately attached to the spirit, we lose touch with our first nature and lose its enormous power to carry us through human fulfillment.

Our successful animal nature is why we live at all in the hostile, physical environments of the planet. To deny or compromise that nature, or to pretend it is otherwise, diminishes the power of that nature to infuse us with the robust presence of lifeforce. The psychosomatic connection is real. Possess an odd idea of your nature, treat yourself accordingly, and you will become a peculiar human, one not likely to survive were you returned to a state of nature.

An open, natural attention to animal matters is not license for brutish, oafish, or socially insensitive behavior. As humans, we can bring a decorum to the subject, even an aesthetic. But first the basic skills are wanted. Among the objects for any dog soldier discipline should be a thorough set of objects pertaining to the demands of our animalness. Those considered by the Manual are feeding, cleanliness, physical tensions, medicines, appearance, hair, apparel, posture and gait, and habitats. Take care of these matters, and everything looks better. If you want to soar like a eagle, tend to your feathers.

Feeding

At bottom, our fate is no different from that of the worm. We must feed the tube. Our life flesh is built out of and fueled by substances found only outside in the environment. So we must ingest matter from the environment, digest its useable ingredients, and eliminate the waste. We feed, therefore, we live.

Most of the hard work of converting the elements of physical matter into the chemistry of organic flesh is done by plants. The animal does not have to search out and consume potassium in mineral form for the plants have already found it and incorporated it into living matter. When the animal eats the plant, the potassium is passed on. This is the classic food chain, where already organically processed matter is passed along among life forms. The herbivore lives by feeding upon the plant kingdom. The carnivore lives by feeding upon the herbivore.

Generally speaking, the greater the diversity of things a species can feed upon and digest, the better the species' survivability. The human has evolved with two feeding natures. One is the solitary, day long, omnivorous, browsing pattern of the primate, with its pronounced sweet tooth. The other is the communal hunt, feast and famine, pattern of the predator, with a metabolism primed by meat. The human can get by on vegetable matter alone, but meat is by far more densely nutritious. We do not digest raw meat all that well, but a well steeped broth can raise us from the dead. What would you think of a chimpanzee that developed an exclusionary attitude toward bananas?

There are three objects to feeding behavior, satisfying the needs of sustenance and nutrition, balancing the energy equation of calories burned versus calories consumed, and achieving consistency throughout ingestion, digestion, and elimination.

Know the important human needs for vitamins, minerals and nutrients, and the foods which amply supply them. Then make sure you eat them, even if only as a pill. In general, if you eat something of everything often enough, and you will get enough of everything.

In the matter of cooking, any dog soldier will be comfortably proficient in the culinary crafts and arts. A man who cannot sensibly and skillfully feed himself has emasculated himself. Good cooking is simple, easy to study and refine, and is essentially a preliminary digestive process that provides for better digestion later, long after the tasty confab is actually eaten. Through use of heat, liquid, and culinary procedures and equipment, the organic matter of meat and plant are broken up and blended together into compositions that have good taste, texture, eye appeal, and easy inner digestion. But unless your teeth have fallen out, always insure that your food takes a good chewing to get it down.

We also eat to fuel the furnaces of animal life. We gain calories from food which we burn to sustain our metabolism and activity. For the lower animals, this mostly entails finding and eating more food, all day long. There are some genetic anomalies that cause excess weight gain, but basically, if you are overweight, you are eating too much and are not active enough. You cannot cheat the calorie equation over the long run. If you take in more calories than you burn, your body will readily store it as fat. The primeval predator faced famine and starvation, and quickly turned the gorging feasts into life sustaining fat. A couple of days later without food found the predator gaunt once more. The human just stays fat.

Know the calories available for given amounts and kinds of foods, and match them with the calorie expenditures created by your activity. The tables and formulas of this knowledge exist in the data banks of modern society and are accessible if you are literate. You should know these things like you know the weight of your car engine's oil and its average miles per gallon. The object is to rationally match over time, your patterns of calorie intake, feeding, with your patterns of calorie consumption, the activities you spend your day in. Your brain does this in gross measure anyway. Work hard, and you become ravenously hunger. Eat little, and your metabolism slows dramatically. Generally speaking, persistent imbalances in the calorie equation, either way, are unhealthy in the long run.

Finally, accept the animal nature of the tube, from mouth to its far end. An experienced hunter can tell a lot from the scat of prey, in particular, what it has been eating, how well that was digested, and the general condition of the animal, its strength or its sickness. You should know the same about yourself. Know the signs of good eating and digesting, and the signs that something is out of balance that needs setting right.

One useful feeding practice when the digestive process becomes chronically imbalanced, or just as a matter of regular routine to gain its beneficial effects, is to fast upon occasion. Animal metabolism builds up a waste residue, much like a car engine's wear pollutes its lubricating oil. Well defined fasting procedures create a drawing action throughout the body, cell by cell, which gives the entire physiology a chance to clean house, reset its settings, and repair what needs fixing. The brain needs this recharge as much as the body. The chemistry of the brain is by far the most complex in the physical being. A simple fast clears the blood, and gives the brain the maintenance time it needs as working organ.

Cleanliness

Even a fly will clean itself. Some animal species have evolved relatively indifferent to filth, but not the human. Our naked skin gives us an intimate awareness of where we stop and where the environment begins. We feel good restoring our selves to the pristine states of cleanliness. Throughout the routines of living and working, the environment rubs all over us. We sweat and secrete in response. When we clean all this wearing away, we recapture the pure feeling of our separate existence from the environment. Many primitive human cultures have had to survive in harsh, uncompromising environments. But with only a few exceptions, in the worst of conditions, none failed to keep themselves reasonably clean.

Besides discouraging the growth of harmful germs and bacteria, being clean and having clean things around you feels good. The skin, in particular, is very responsive to regular bathing and to contact with things clean to the touch. The skin both breathes and secretes over every square inch of its extent. Vigorously cleaning and rubbing the skin, including the scalp, shines the mind and soothes the emotion, even if just for a few moments.

Cleanliness extends beyond the physical person, and includes clothes, possessions and habitat. Keeping all this clean becomes work, requiring discipline and attention. There is never any call to take an objective to the extreme, as obsession or fetish, but sensible standards of cleanliness, and the behaviors which achieve them, are a necessary part of the dog soldier's lifestyle. It is simply taking proper care of what you are and what you have.

Physical Tensions

One consequence of an active, striving animal life is the appearance of many little physical tensions that get stored in the body. If allowed to add up, these tensions can leave us wadded up, like a puppet with all its strings pulled too tight. We twist up inside in fixed, narrow ways, and eventually our body language shows it. Our postures, faces, and gait look cramped, cringing, or gnarled. If you fail to handle the daily proliferation of physical tension, the psychosomatic connection eventually points our your failure with ulcers, strokes, heart attacks and the like.

We try hard. Modern society sets many demanding tasks before us. When we fail to take care of them, bad things happen. So we set up our tasks and chores like prey animals, and plunge through them with the unrelentingly tenseness of purpose of a starving predator. Succeed or fail, we end up carrying the track of our intentions and drives, our psychic commitment to the hunt, in our muscles and nerves. Any ordinary day in the life can leave you with tensions strung throughout your body like little knots, tangles, and twists that must be untied and released as a part of the daily animal routine.

Animals are remarkably adept at handling the business of combatting these residues of intensity. Both dogs and cats have elaborate stretching, shivering, and yawning behaviors, and most instructively, they engage in these behaviors as long as they sense that it is necessary. These natural remedies are available to the human, but we tend to inhibit them instead of encouraging and developing them. Consequently, more deliberating means are necessary for managing human tensions.

Most physical conditioning regimes work well, as their thorough employment of the whole body finally washes away the petty tensions in floods of sheer extended exertion. But as the petty tensions exist physically, they can also be found, one by one, through attention, free form stretching, Tai Chi like in its patience in finding where the knot lies, and gradually letting it untie itself, then release into the body as new smoothing motions. Dance also works wonders in wiping the body free of its little tensions, and is a uniquely human response to the physical stress problem. Self dancing in private is a useful art in cleansing the musculature of its nervous twitches.

Massaging practices produce much the same effect. Self massaging jaws, sinuses, limbs, temples, joints and other physical parts breaks up the cysts of tension, and leaves the body free for a moment from the psychosomatic connection. Hot baths, cold showers, even intense music loving, will send cascading shivers throughout your body, and break up the knots of animal tension.

The face, in particular, deserves special treatment. As much cerebral cortex is devoted to the control of the face as is devoted to the rest of the body, and we work it a hundred different ways every day. Tension and fatigue built up in the face and drag it down. Use your hands and fingers to feel, stroke, and gently massage all over your face in soothing ways. Splash your face and eyes with cold water often. Sometimes just close your eyes and rest all those facial muscles at once in quiet repose.

There is another source of tension besides striving that can become just as dysfunctional as the tension from dynamic behavior. We can inhibit action with the same intensity we show when we strive. We hold back urges and restrain our behavior. Instead of expressing, we suppress, and if too much practiced, we constipate ourselves, mentally, physically, and emotionally. A lively physical conditioning practice usually prevents this side of tension from developing in extreme, but it is worth noting the reappearing role of the animal tube. The actual rhythm and nature of ingestion, digestion, and elimination often reflects the rhythms of action, inhibition, and release that we experience in daily work and living. Learn to relax when there is time to relax. Let rest come naturally, not according to schedule.

Generally, work hard when work needs to be done. Play hard and enjoy life when the hard work has created the boon of leisure. No man is a robot or a machine. Good use of downtime is a serious survival skill. Without time for the natural regenerative processes of the physiology to work its wonders, we grind down, wear out too soon, age prematurely, and eventually breakdown.

Medicines, Pallatives, and Doctors

The well conditioned human body resists disease, prevents injuries, and heals well. But since the beginning, homo sapiens have combed the natural environment to find and extract substances that aid, even cure, the maladies and ailments that may plague the living human. Medicine may be the first real science of the species, and appears indigenously wherever human culture shows up. No human culture fails to develop its own arts of medicine out of what the surrounding natural environment provides. The idea behind medicine is simple. We deliberately ingest refined, external substances for the purpose of affecting interior states for the better, especially when those interior states have fallen below normal, or become deficient in some way, like gas, headaches, fevers, colds, rashes, and the like.

Through trial and error, and empirical observation, distinctive medicines emerge that reliably produce positive effects in given situations. But we only gain the positive effects by trying causes, and this implies risk. Often negative effects will appear as well, and the net effect varies widely between human to human. You have to study the effect of ingested substances carefully. What works for others may not work as well for you.

Concerning the matter of drugs. America is the aficionado's drug culture. We have pills and capsules for fifty seven varieties of headaches, bad gas, heartburn, indigestion, muscle aches, joint aches, whole body aches, neuralgia, allergies, liver ailments, vitamin supplements, herbal concoctions, diarrhea, constipation, congestion, insomnia, you name it, there is a pill you can take. There a hundreds of thousands of prescriptions filled each year for anti-depressants and tranquilizers. This may have something to do with why polls show Americans more optimistic than they have been for decades. We are not much smarter, but we are a whole lot more drugged.

In our defense, we might blame the hard drinking rites of our old frontier. Even Washington nursed himself through the cold nights of war with a bottle or two of madeira wine. Drinking a man under the table was an old Western method of character testing. Drugs like alcohol both stimulate and depress the controlling nervous system. They amplify and exaggerate tendencies. Even when there was no law, no paper and ink, no judges or lawyers, deals still had to be made, mano a mano. Drink hard with a man and something of their inner nature was revealed. How would they behave under stress? How did they behave when in their cups? Goofy? Belligerent? Stupid? Repetitve? Or was a hard will hanging on and handling the licker?

The dog soldier's tool kit contains a personal medicine kit. Our metabolisms slip out or kilter often, and we experience the symptoms of discomfort, ill feelings and petty pains. It is neither wise or necessary to suffer these afflictions when simple, medicinal applications will relieve the negative effects of the malady. Failing to treat a wound is not macho. It is stupid.

The same general process of learning applies to medicines, pallatives, ointments and ablations, as applies to all objects of personal grooming. Pay attention to causes, observe effects, trust your native intelligence, and act according to what you learned. This includes vitamins, bioenzymes, hormones, diets, as well as prescription and over the counter drugs. Develop a keen inner perception of what you sense to be normal health and hold on to it. Let go of the medicine when you return to normal and watch out for unfavorable tradeoffs. Side effects that leave you outside normal feeling can offset, or even be worse, than the relief you gain from allieviating the original symptoms.

For tough cases, all cultures have invented the profession of the doctor, be it witch doctor or health maintenance organization. Even at the tribal level, the business of physiological benefits derived from external substances becomes too complex and extensive for each individual to learn as part of their basic cultural competence. The accomplishments of the modern society's medical profession passes beyond the astonishing to the miraculous. All the more reason to issue a pair of cautions concerning doctors.

First, despite the impressive science and technology, doctors are still human, the same kind of human that once religiously bled patients for all manner of ailment, killing some, and speeding the demise of many others. This despite the invariable weakening effect of leaching upon the physiology that is universally observable. This blood sucking stupidity, which killed of George Washington before he had a chance to recover, is a case of too much theory and not enough empirical sense.

Always make the doctor explain everything that questions your mind, and insist upon it until you are sure in your understanding of what is being diagnosed, its causes, the treatment and its theory, and the prognosis. Medical knowledge is specialized, not incomprehensible. If your doctor cannot teach you all the why's and wherefore's of your medical condition, they may not really understand what they are doing. Keep your own empirical sense as to what you are really feeling and the effects you perceive occurring in you, sharp and free of prejudice or suggestion. What the doctor says should be happening, or what you hope is happening, may not be what you are really sensing. Good practices of health are important, but first you need a clear and true sense of what good health feels like.

Second, despite the fact that doctors value the role of a robust physical life in preventing illness and speeding recovery, they tend to take a passive view of treatment, physically passive from your point of view. Sometimes a direct, behavioral response is more sensible. A personal anecdote illustrates. Once, after a period of too many soft burgers and casseroles, I developed a large lump below and beside my lower, leftside incisor. The dentist's X-ray showed a huge black void, an abscess. The tooth was hardly alive electrically, and noticeably wiggled if tested. The recommended course of action was a referral to an oral surgeon and a thousand dollars of root canal and bridgework.

But upon thinking about it, I could see that the tooth and others nearby had been suffering from a neglect of basic function. So I bought some gum and began chewing, chewing even on the washcloth to get a workout in, buying carrots and chewy meat to add to my diet. In two weeks, the abscess was gone, the tooth firm, and no problems for ten years. Gum disease succumbs to the same regime. Vigorously massage them with fingers and terrycloth, and chew with determination.

To reinforce the point, a recent study showed that middle aged and elderly people who started specifically exercising their pelvic muscles, suddenly experienced a significant reduction in incontinence, if not its disappearance. Lose touch with the body and it will oblige and fall asleep on you, for so many years that it forgets to function at all. This is the fate of the drone, not the dog soldier. Do not accept passive treatment when a common sense behavioral response to the malady is obvious and within your competence to perform with discipline.

Finally, there is the matter of the warrior's ablutions. Soldiers and warriors of all manner throughout human culture and history engage in extensive preparations upon the eve of battle to ready themselves for the effort and the challenge. Many of these rituals and behavioral self programming involve systematic assaults upon the physiology, like fasting, dancing, special meals or smokes, sweat lodges, personal rites of meditations, or stimulating ointments and war paint. There would be no such a pronounced, universal culture in these physiological preparations precurrent to peak performance if they did not create actual performance advantages when execution is on the line, when the stakes are high, and the risks of failure considerable.

If the performance is important, ablutions and rites of preparation that concentrate and set the whole being, mind, body, and soul, upon that performance are a sensible and intelligent part of the performance itself. If the deed matters, set your focus and ready yourself.

Appearance

It is not the position of the Manual to tell any man how they should look. To invite conformity while professing freedom would be inconsistent. But the most prevalent trend in the male culture of modern society has been one of emasculation. Male fashions are dull, stiff, shapeless, and ugly in color. Consequently, the Manual will spend some effort in countering this trend in an attempt to restore sense and naturalness to the expression of male appearance.

Our physical appearances, our looks, our corporal presence, and our movements, are the visual signatures of our identity in the minds and memories of others. When others form pictures of us, our physical appearances is what they see. Some of our physical attributes we can do little about, but there is much we can and do. In a culture of freedom, a wide range of fashion and otherwise quite original appearances will show up.

Amid all the variations possible in your appearance, and the different aesthetics implied, there is really only one criterion that matters. Can you live with your ways of appearance? Can you accept their costs and consequences? Are you really comfortable in them? Or are you trapped in them?

Whether you pay attention or not, the development of appearance is a selective process. We choose one look over others, and that choice and that appearance becomes us, at least outwardly. Some thought, care, and purpose at this is not only logical, but is an affirmation of self and personal legend. Like it or not, our personal visage is a direct function of personal choice. Few things so intimately define us.

Some will always find us wanting on some pretext or another. But when differences in appearance are taken as empirical evidence of superiority, the European Social Disease is at work. When the wisdom, "Do not judge a book by its cover", was phrased, it was not to warn us about books, but to warn us that you cannot know the true worth of a man by his outward appearances.

One inviolate dog soldier trust is to never use dress or appearance to project airs of superiority or dominance. Nor grant such to the designer frabricated. It is not the color of money in looks and appearance that matters, but the personal thought, creativity, and grooming showing through. You do not have to be plain like a monk to be common with the people.

Mostly we are just different in appearance, largely in seeming animal type. We look like bears, stallions, and wolves, sometimes like eagles and panthers. But mostly we just look different. Deal with it. Tolerate it.

While none of us can do all that much about the animal looks nature has given us, we can cultivate a healthy, graceful body, and a warm face given often to smiles and good humor. After that, make it a personal object to study the different appearances that make up the wardrobes of your life. Turn the perplexities of appearance into a craft of personal theater. Stay reasonably critical of the results and allow yourself to move through styles of appearances as the roles in your life are called upon stage. Usually simple, natural approaches to appearance hold up the best and need the least maintenance. You want to be in command of your looks, not their slave.

Hair

The Cheyenne used to beg the white chiefs to let their soldiers grow their hair long so that there might be honor in killing them. On the other hand, the Cheyenne did not have to face the morning rites of razor sharp shaves, or the tedium of primping and trimming overgrown facial hair. Neither did Cheyenne comprehend what male pattern baldness and trench warfare could do to the male psyche.

Hair presents a difficult prescription. Not only do the physical characteristics of hair differ widely within the species, the customs on how to handle male hair vary considerably across cultural contexts. Both scalp and facial hair can be alternately long, full, contoured, braided, greased, oiled, shaved, shortened, flat topped, mohawked, waved or left unkept, with a fair amount of tedium involved in keeping up any style and approach, save the slovenly.

The Manual offers two, somewhat competing, objects concerning male hair, and otherwise leaves this problem in personal originality to the individual dog soldier. Let the natural qualities of your hair guide you, yet keep the whole business convenient.

Human hair stands out from the animal kingdom in three remarkable ways. It varies wildly across the species, it grows and grows without sensible limit, and we have to sleep on it. If left to grow without tending, human hair turns each of us into the unmistakable animal that we are, and can become a royal pain in the ass to take care of.

The naturalness that is best for you is hard to judge. You have to grow your hair out once, long and full, to observe and know its nature, before you can decide how you will handle it. Generally speaking, natural aesthetics are easier to maintain, and seem to fit best with the rest of your physical makeup. Naturally displayed human hair reinforces our unique corporal identity, no less signifying us as do our faces. Would you undergo plastic surgery to remove all the distinctive features of your face? You gain, rather than lose, a new signification of male being when you let your hair be what it will.

Male hair is one of our most potent expressions of our specialized gender. Be wary of approaches that emasculate without practical cause. There is no compelling reason why the ears should get cold and the back of the neck chilly. Nor any compelling reason why hair should get in the way and become a bother.

The natural aesthetic must be kept in proper perspective. There are matters of use and function to be considered. Seasons change from hot to cold. Certain lines of works and activity benefit from more functional approaches. Helmets and other head gear are more comfortable in use when the hair is shaped to suit the equipment. Then there is the matter of simple economy. The care and upkeep of the hair should be simple and convenient. The female of the species may need to indulge the tediums of refined hair design, but the male should have better things to do.

A peculiar modern styling in male hair makes a good illustration how these competing objects of naturalness and convenience come into play. There is a custom among the well heeled drone, or aspiring politician, to vaccuform their hair, every hair in its place and in its correct color of shade, all air brushed perfectly and molded into an eternal appearance, like a wig, as if hair never grew or showed any life to it.

This styling is neither natural or convenient. The hair appears pressed into a shape that is then stamped upon the skull like a prayer cap, looking the same as it always has, hour by hour, day by day, photograph by photograph. Hair takes the same ride through life our face and our body takes. The seasons will show unless we artificially fake things. Trying to keep the hair fixed and immutable when everything else about us physically is changing and maturing is odd and rather silly.

The vaccuformed hair style is also inconvenient. It takes precision hands to cut and trim, and frequent visits to the same to hide the fact that hair sweats, preens, and actually grows. This is expensive and takes something of a fetish to keep up the appearance. The cost becomes one of those demarcations that those with really superior airs use to separate themselves from the common people who cannot afford such contrivance. If they are to flaunt their ability to indulge extravagance in hair, they should seek a more artful model, like Louis, the 14th.

If left on their own and to their own devices, the competent dog soldier will be able to cut and shape their own hair as needed, and make it look good.

Apparel

Clothes and personal adornments have also been too often employed by those determined to enforce and perpetuate social standing. What you wear is expected to mark your rank in the hierarchy. The French aristocrat, or the British, must contrive to perfect the human peacock fashion, while the peasants, the lower classes, were expected to dress frumpy and dreary, as befits their small, poor station. Such considerations are irrelevant to the dog soldier.

Clothes first of all should satisfy the practical requirements of the occasion. To be dressed inadequately to the demands of the exposure and the environment is to betray lack of foresight and prudence. Keep your raiment clean, mended, and in repair. Take advantage of the sheddable nature of clothes, and use a change of clothing to set the occasion for new activities and new scenes, from work to play, from lounging about to stepping out. All clothes are costumes. Dress and adorn for the roles you would play. The theater in life is easy to craft and makes ordinary living more enjoyable and more interesting to live.

Allow yourself to dress in natural, comfortable, unconstricting ways. It is one of the strange curiosities of the modern civilized drone, fully blessed like all human males with an Adam's Apple and full chest, to then don apparel which chokes and constricts the throat, impeding the natural rhythms of breathing.

The irony of the tie choker and the sack suit is that both mimic in a bland, denatured way, original displays of fashion that were intended to openly emphasize male sexuality, just as women are allowed to emphasize their sexuality with makeup, nylons, and high heels. The tie is the sorry, vestigial remnant of a long tradition of drawing the eye to the unquestionably male sexual characteristic of a broad and hairy chest. The ruffled lace, the silk scarves and gold chains pronounced the male gender. The reason the parson wore the Roman collar was to signify their contrasting sexual safety and impotence. Only the modern tie remains of this old display, a loose, limp flap of artificial skin, a long dead albatross, dangling close enough to the loins for the insecure male's fingers to unconsciously touch and fondle.

The Puritan, ready to be buried in, sack suit, represents a similar denaturing. It mocks the military uniform, but without the color, the bold cuts and lines, and the trim and insignia that make military garb striking to the eye. The sack suit cult appears based upon an aesthetic bent on destroying masculine originality, making all politically correct males look as if they were each cut from the same drab cloth, in the same dull style, all pressed into the same stiff shape that totally obfuscates the male form. Some how this cardboard flat appearance is thought to engender trust and to project respectability and authority. Like the Emperor's new clothes, see through these airs. Clothes may make the picture of the man, but they have little to do with the actual making of the man.

To choose at all in what one wears, when and how, is to reveal a personal aesthetic, a signature pattern of color, form, design and decoration. Do not let the aesthetic develop by default. Consider it and decide what you like. Let clothes express your original identity, the whole point of your human existence. No human is so creatively deficient as to be incapable of finding the distinct touches, and the unique combinations of appearance, that mark them as original, interesting to look at, and even attractive. There is nothing wrong with men dressing in ways that complement their sense of sensuality and their sexual nature. Unless, of course, you want only drones.

Posture and Gait

The contribution to personal appearance made by apparel and adornment, however, is largely passive. Two very important active objects must also be given attention, good posture and a smooth, easy gait.

The Protestant Zealots of Europe pioneered stiff, uptight practices in posture and gait. All sitting was squared off in rigid, right angles. Even with wide, downy mattresses and warm flowing comforts, the Puritans slept at attention. Most of the rest of the world and the rest of human history practiced easy, natural lounging or sitting, and balanced that with energetic behavior when on their feet.

Bipedal locomotion is what made the human species what it is today. The erect spine, with the upward and outward looking head, is our natural posture. But it is easy for soft, modern humans to give into gravity, and habitually bend over, eyes scarcely looking above eye level if up at all. Stretch out and wriggle the spine, reaching for all your height, head and chin up, until all the skeletal structure, so well designed to stand fully upright, settles and aligns naturally. This feels good, is good for you, and brings on better sleep. It also prepares the body for any and all important movements. This simple, regular exercise of your natural physique keeps your postures natural and easy to put into motion. If you do not daily fight the battle against gravity, you will end up crab like and stunted in later age.

Likewise, a strong, fluid, and outward flowing gait, one that could go on for miles, is both healthy and attractive. We became biped not to stand or shuffle about, but to run, leap, and stroll. A successful gait is one which can adeptly break into a run, or a trot, or a sudden move with apparent ease and sureness.

Can you walk with a book placed square atop your head without jarring it free? Can you confidently walk a balance beam, even at ground level? When you run, can you run in all kinds of different ways, dodging here and there, making each step a unique spontaneous challenge in balance, footing, and momentum? Many joggers, while improving upon the lazy boy life, do themselves no real favors when they run in repetitive, stereotypic forms, over and over. One slight twist and the narrowly worked bones, ligaments, and muscles are caught in angles and stresses they have no conditioning to prepare them for. Like a carpal tunnel syndrome for joggers. When you move, let your whole body participate in the activity, not just narrow segments of it. Move like a cat, not insect like, like some beetle.

Finally, when free to lounge, lounge. Explore the more luxurious stretchings and relaxings of the physical being. A physique that must on occasion bear the stress of hard, narrow force and movement needs to experience and enjoy the opposite physical state, that of the fluid and spreading comfort found in lounging. The Ancient Romans, who built the first empire to offer universal citizenship, had the natural rhythms of motion well defined and down pat. When they were on their feet, they marched to the beat of accomplishment. But when they were free to rest, they got off their feet, laid out horizontally on their couches, and lounged freely like lions in the summer grass.

Habitat Maintenance

It is not in the nature of the predator to foul its own nest. This is the difference betweeen the dog and the pig. Dogs can be house broken. They instinctually respect the sanctity of the den. The pig cannot. Bad smells will bother a dog. One of the biological advantages of the pig is that no smell will deter it from food. How we shape and maintain our habitat, where we live, is a direct expression of who we are. The dog soldier keeps a smart camp, ship shape.

Few dog soldiers will ever face the burden of furnishing a mansion. One must strive to make good, effective use of the spaces and resources available. You want your habitat to suit and support your favorite behavior patterns, your activities, your projects, your amusements, even hospitality if you are so fortunate to have friends who visit. You want your habitat to also efficiently handle and support the normal, but necessary domestic operations any human living in modern society must carry out routinely to live decently, operations like trash disposal, cooking, laundry, food procurement and storage, media connections, and the like.

Put serious thought into how you design and shape the various functional aspects of your habitat, that base of operations that makes up your daily living environment. How do you set up the biological regulation room, what hygienic tools and ablutions do you need arranged for regular, easy use? What feeding patterns does your kitchen need to support? How do you dress your sleeping quarters or arrangements? How do you locate and organize the devices of technology you choose to employ? Where do you read, or think, or center your feelings? What patterns of living do you require?

But be more creative than brute function. Consider how your habitat could look. Decorate your mileau through personal touches that please you. You should like just looking around your quarters because all that you see carries your personal signature, in every piece, in every position, next to everything else. Even if spartan or spare, there are always compelling aesthetics to find, and interesting, yet effective arrangements to make. When enough seasons weather the premises, change over the face of your living arrangements. Unchanging environments become stale, and soon do we.

But no matter how attractive and pleasant one can make their surroundings, ordinary living and use disarrange and clutter. Systems of regular cleaning, restoration, and maintenance, driven by need and a manifest sense of quality, must be developed and regularly carried out to keep up a habitat as it should be.

No obsessions or fetishes are wanted. One sensibly maintains one's habitat to live and work in comfortably, conveniently, and effectively, whether to feed, rejuvenate, or deal officially with the outer world and its demanding institutions. You keep your habitat clean and ordered, in order to enjoy its use. This means living in it, not visiting it.

There is no men's work, no women's work, only work that has to be done. When we clean, arrange, and improve our living conditions, we do something for ourselves, where no selfishness against others can possibly be involved. When we secure our home, where we must live, day in and day out, we become a little stronger when we face outward again, toward the world of other people, reality, and Mother Nature. We are more ready to face and fend off the slings and arrows of outrageous fortune when we have a place ready to receive us when the day is finally called and we retire from the field.

Remember that where you are, in any present moment, is essentially your habitat. Make a contribution wherever it is needed, or suggests itself.

A Specimen Daily Program of Anima Hygiene

What is offered here is intended only as an illustration. Dog soldier discipline is not a matter of the religious observance of a fixed set of chores and duties, motions to go through, forms to conform to. A really active, interesting life will interfere anyway.

The observance of practice is for the purpose of readiness, not propriety. The key is to understand and stay focused on the objects involved and the benefits they yield. Through paying attention, we become aware of hygienic deficits and can act directly to bring them up to par.

Bathe, rub skin vigorously, wash hair, and massage scalp.

Brush, pick, and rub teeth and gums vigorously.

Rinse eyes and face often.

Work the eyeballs, especially while holding a visual lock. This trains the visual cortex as well as the eye muscles.

Eat at least one good meal a day, and rest well
afterwards.

Bite hard and chew thoroughly.

Sleep, nap, or rest as needed.

Breathe in fresh air and sunshine, or whatever exposure the weather provides.

Exercise,limber and stretch.

Evacuate the bowels at least once.

Laugh often, from the belly, if possible.

Wash and massage the feet.

Pick up or clean portions of your habitat.

Think.

Enjoy something and someone enormously.

Do a good thing, however little, especially for a stranger in an unexpected way.

Reflect upon the fact that the real miracle is that
you are here to experience the good of feeling good at all.

Worldly Affairs

We live in dual worlds, the world of nature and animal survival, and the world of mammon and social standing. Unlike the monk, the dog soldier trains to live in the real world as it is, and among the people as they are. If the world holds dangers, risks, temptations and disappointments, it also holds the challenges and adversities that become the stuff a dog soldier is made for.

The point of dog soldier discipline is to make changes in ourselves for the better that also make a real difference in how our worldly affairs go, not just for ourselves, but for others as well, be they close in the kinship, or just another frequent stranger. The Manual considers among worldly affairs those objects of discipline that fall within provinces of nature, mammon, government, cultural competence, possessions, manners, conduct, fortune and failure, and personal legend.

Nature

The human species spawned in nature. This land, sky, and sea, with its abundant life and turbulent weather, all that reigns upon the planet surface, that is our breeding ground. We can survive well in nature because we were bred from nature to live within it. The real surprise is that we can adapt as well as we do to the artificial, manufactured worlds frenetic civilization creates.

Nature is both boon and bane. All the sources of our material existence arise in nature. We get air to breath, water to drink, and food and shelter from a provident, life giving nature. Through our sciences, we have gotten nature to yield the even greater bounties that fuel civilization. We make steel, electricity, and bricks, and build our world of mammon in impressive style in nature's midst, almost at times as if in seeming defiance of nature.

For nature also brings earthquakes, tornadoes, droughts, floods, plagues, pestilence, and the iron laws of physics and gravity. The same mother that feeds the lifeforce of the species, places that life at risk. We can build stairs to live above the ground, and fall down them and break our necks. Odd how some forget natural reality and drive as if safe at any speed. Or walk out into the wilderness as if no more risk or danger were at hand than an excursion through a shopping mall harbors.

The dog soldier will have a healthy respect for the risks and realities of nature. Nature is quite unforgiving when we mistake her. The old rules of survival still apply. The better we comprehend and appreciate nature, the better our choices and chances will be.

A respect for nature is really a respect for our origins. Very positive connections still exist, even as we hide away in our interior rooms of modern society. To move within the spaces of primal nature, be it in a park, or under the shade of a tree, draws us out of our minds into the immediate present of sensation and perception, of spontaneous action. Even a little exposure to nature, its fresh airs, brisk winds, its distant horizons and far vistas, its rising crescent moons, and the brilliance of sunshine breaking through high, rippled clouds like a mother of pearl rainbow, or seeping into a sunset like flames die into embers, these experiences stimulate and enliven us fully and deeply, in a way nothing else can. Communing with nature is simple and evokes a good sense of being, the reassuring feeling only the natural environment can stir. For a moment we are home, and every animal sense we possess is aware of it.

But just being outside physically, moving station to station, or touring scenic spots, is not enough. You want to engage yourself totally in the experience, to sink into the open spaces, to sense and see the teeming life, to attune your inner rhythms to the feeling nature envokes. If your head and eyes are not up and searching all that vision supplies, noticing its detail and wondering on its origins, you are behaving as you would were you inside the squared off cubes of the cell block hives. Nature uplifts us and clarifies the consciousness like the sweetness of a clear mountain stream. The dog soldier lives first in nature, avidly studying its ways, and finally, dies in nature, eyes searching the four directions until the last to see what nature still beholds.

Of special importance are the rhythms and seasons of nature, for these are always the rhythms of work and play that we are most comfortable living in. Natural life is a symphony of rhythm. When we fall out of rhythm, we feel out of sorts, beside ourselves, or just plain rode hard and put away wet. Civilization creates many artificial rhythms. At one end, through schedules, alarms, and daily planners, we can regiment ourselves as efficiently as a robot might. At the other end, we can go off the clock entirely, as one finds in the eternal present of a Las Vegas casino. Not surprisingly, when we try to tie our natural, inner, biorhythms to these artificial rhythms, we eventually lose touch with the inner rhythms, or crack up wildly out of balance. When we put our biorhythms in time with the naturally occurring rhythms of the environment, we find work less wearing, and rest, more soothing and rejuvenating.

Mammon

Then there is the burgeoning world of maddening crowds manufactured by civilization, mammon, the world of property, towns, possessions, governments, taxes and laws, sundry social institutions, money, technology, motivated economic activity, social standing and politics, the media, airports, cities, suburbs, and ghettos, all teeming with people, mostly strangers, some good, some bad. Mammon, like nature, can be boon or bane, a matter of tradeoffs.

The human ability to form and manage cooperative, collective enterprises has led to extraordinary accomplishments in the sciences and technologies of material well being and social organization. The refinements and progress of human culture has taken much of the brutish, nasty, and short out of human life.

Human moral progress is less impressive. Some broad improvements are noteworthy. We do not condone slavery anymore, or publically torture and execute deviants, and have at least published bills of the rights and freedoms of the common man, even incorporated them into actual constitutions of government. But human culture, the close in, scene to scene, breaking of actual human social behavior, comes with all the imperfections of the species. These flaws create the ragged edges and internal hemorrhages of modern society. Not everything goes well for everyone. Some cross into crime. Others suffer injustice stoically, with no recourse or defense. Some twist and cave in to nirvanic drugs like cocaine and heroin. Some grow up in abject poverty, viciously abusive homes, or ridiculous affluence.

Greed is unreproached, and selfishness an asset to civilized success. Many are discriminated against still on the basis of gender or apparent race, when all they want to do is be the best they can be like anybody else. The European Social Disease and Social Darwinism creep up everywhere like a nasty, recurring flu epidemic, creating lots of ill feelings, resentments, envies, and anti-social vanities. Partisan zealots, Right or Left, fight like roosters in a cock fight to gain the levers of governmental power to enforce their ideologically pure and politically correct social agenda on the people, complete with sanctions and punitive police powers, invariably limiting, restricting, or eliminating rights and freedoms once enjoyed without fetter. Who in Mammon will tolerate human freedom, when it is possible to organize and fix the matter?

Monks and anchorites can flee the insanities of civilization and seek some saintly, greater life apart. But the dog soldier must live among the people. The greater life must be won where it is hardest fought, among the people in the world of mammon. Indeed, far from rejecting the world of material things and organized society, the dog soldier is free to win the game by its own rules, if that seems a relevant ambition. It is not the gains and successes of your individual endeavors that matters so much as does what you do with it. Without bond to kinship, there can be no dog soldier. If you achieve material success, and can help lots and lots of others, many of whom will actually turn out to be good people, and really make a difference in the quality of their lives, you have earned the eagle feathers of a chieftain's headdress. But do not forget the lots and lots part. Material success should widen the field of honor and noble actions.

Remember the wisdom of the Cheyenne. Let your generosity, virtue, and well meaningness bind the kinship to your lead. But leave them free of coercion, threat, or presumed obligation. Success is a matter of fortune. But freedom is a cooperative attainment, the finest any social organization can achieve, be it the size of a lion's pride, or a swarming modern megapolis.

In the wilderness of mammon, survival comes through vigilance, discipline, education, perseverance, but especially through successful kinship cooperations. Mammon is a world of risk and opportunity. It is a world where fortune can defeat merit and elevate the lucky miscreant. In Mammon, evil prospers, the wicked go unpunished, and all is vanity under the sun. Injustice and wrong happen daily and without warning. Good people are stymied or injured. Common people are exploited and oppressed, and any of us are liable to catch a bad run of luck at the hands of others. This is the field upon which the charge, to protect and defend, must be played out. This is where the dog soldier makes a difference. The people never have too many dog soldiers.

Government

When the human science of agriculture finally matured 12,000 years ago, food surplus was produced in record quantities. Crafts and trade flourished. Bureaucracy organized. The number of human beings that could live together as one social organization grew far beyond the typical tribal populations of several hundred. Villages of a thousand sprang up. Some grew into cities of tens of thousands. A few of these learned how to organize armies and grew into nations. The effective simplicity possible in tribal governance necessarily gave way to much more formal and complicated methods of government. The idea of a State, ordered by impersonal law, evolved in human culture.

We know very little about the human dramas that occurred over the long transition from the precepts of tribal governance to the Nation State. No epics, novels, or tragedies have come down to us. The great change in human fortunes took place before the dawn of literacy. When the State appeared 5,000 years ago, it was complete and in charge of the history's record keeping.

Virtually all early states employed the monarchy concept, combined with king worship, to effect and maintain formal government. Sometimes a god was the king's main backer. Sometimes the god was his father. Sometimes the king was the god. The individual rights and freedoms of the tribal setting disappeared in favor of the overpreening power of the State and its neurotic need to order and fix everything to its purposes.

But human cooperative instincts have 100,000 years of tribal conditioning and kinship selection working in them. The first runs of civilization failed to completely rub out the original programming. The Greeks, moving out of the tribal reaches of Archaic Europe and settling on the fringes of the civilized, Middle Eastern Empires, civilized themselves quickly, but kept alive in their charters of government, the individual rights and freedoms of the tribe. They choose to continue making their political decisions by democratic vote as a formal method of achieving the sense of significant consensus that ruled the tribe. The Romans modified these ideas in a Republican Government, and rode the energies it released to a world empire. Whereupon the problem of social organization became too big and too complicated. Rome reverted to old style monarchy under the new name of emperor. But the tribal heritage was persevered in the idea of citizenship. All Roman citizens were equal before the law, once they managed to attain such social standing.

When the Roman Empire fell and Europe descended into the Dark Ages, the barbarian tribes that rebuilt the fabric of Europe forsook their tribal roots, and emulated the Roman Kings they had destroyed. Between the Dark Ages of ignorance, the ascendancy of a dogmatic Church, and the feudal model of government, there were no more attempts at incorporating the tribal ideals of individual rights and freedom into the manifestations of State. The mere discussion of ideas outside the status quo and the orthodoxy, let alone their insistence, could lead to the infernos of the stake, and other ugly forms of public murder. The line of the Ancients Greeks and Romans finally snuffed out. The great heresy of human freedom survived in another cultural line altogether, one almost eradicated by the Romans.

Out of the same ancient heart of Europe from which the Greeks sprang, the Celts appeared, moving westward in large waves of tribes. Around 300 B.C., when Rome finally conquered Italy, the Celts occupied Northern Europe. The Celts are one of the most curious of human cultures to emerge any where in human history. They were strong, fierce warriors with bronze swords, but as infantry, no poor competition for the horse soldiers of Scythia. The Celts had been driven west to find a new homeland, much like the Cheyenne would face 2,000 years later.

The Celts were an imaginative, mystic, and intensely individualistic people. They were long haired, high spirited, and hung the severed heads and skulls of their enemies from the manes of their horses. To the Celts, we owe the legend of Merlin, faire tales, the myths of leprechauns and banshees, Druid princesses and wizards, and Stonehenge. They painted their faces and adorned their bodies for war according to individual rites and revelations. Like the Cheyenne, they celebrated individual deeds and acts of heroism in songs, dance, and celebrations.

The Celts governed themselves in the primal pattern of the nomadic tribe, much like the Cheyenne. They made up their own minds and followed the leaders that inspired them. Little remains of the Celtic occupation of Western Europe. They built with wood, and only shaped the earth. They had no stone walls or buildings of brick. The sense of impermanence was calculated. The Celts came out of the moving spirit of nature and were always ready to move again as one people to occupy and live in new lands.

Reared to the rules of single, personal combat, the Celtic warriors were no match for the organized legions of Julius Caesar, with their iron swords, group tactics, engineering train, and political cunning. Caesar defeated each of the petty Celtic chieftains in detail. When the Celts finally caught on to what was happening, they rose as one people under a popular war chief, Vercingetorix. But Caesar outfoxed his opponent, captured him through a brilliant engineering siege, and had Vercingetorix straggled in Rome as the marquis event of his victory celebration. The Celtic homelands were incorporated into the Roman Province of Gaul.

Rome pursued its conquest of the Celtic culture by invading the Isle of Britannia, establishing one more subsidiary of the Roman Empire. The only Celtic people to escape Romanization were the Irish, the Cornish, the Welsh, and the Scottish, all pushed into rugged lands they could defend bitterly to the end. The Romans were content to wall them off, with real bricks and mortar.

1,600 years later, nestled among these surviving Celtic enclaves, in Northern England not far from William Wallace's sack of York, John Locke, a philosopher, published his treatises on free, popular government. A hundred years later, in the same region, Adam Smith published his tome on free market economy. As if spontaneously regenerated after lying dormant and suppressed for thousands of years, the genie of human freedom was once again released and free to work its powerful magic.

The dream was fulfilled in the American Revolution. The founding Fathers were steeped in Locke. Locke had reached back, mostly by guesswork, to what he called the State of Nature, essentially the tribal environment of human society. In the pristine vision, Locke found the condition of individual human freedom present in all humans, hence their natural political equality. But successful cooperative efforts produce far more benefits and security than individuals can produce on their own. This is the fundamental motive for governance, to get the group to work as an ordered whole to reap the benefits of collective enterprise. The boons of successful social organization are enormous, and its opposite, anarchy, a travesty, a waste, and a terror.

So an intelligent people will bring into the kinship the concept of the social contract, whereby each individual gives up some freedoms, and grants authority to some structure of governance, in order to secure the boons of social organization for all. This is what Lincoln reduced to perfect clarity when he said, "Of the people, by the people, and for the people". Locke went further, though, and laid the foundations and motives for political revolution. The kinship is not bound over to governance for the sake of government. The goal of the social contract is to secure the better fruits of social organization, stability, providence, and justice, and above all, the preservation of human freedoms. When these goals are forgotten, and only the laws are remembered, government begins to go bad. When segments of the people are oppressed, when injustice flourishes, when great inequities in wealth exist, when privilege and standing are above the law, the social contract is breached and betrayed. Since the social contract is initiated through the motives of the people to combine, they are free, and fully invested with the right, to dissolve and reconstitute the framework of their governance.

Yet in the capstones of Locke's heresy, the American Revolution and the U.S. Constitution, the foundations of individual freedom were nearly lost. The inclusion of the Bill of Rights was a close call. And as predicted by the forefathers, this charter as been chipped away at and compromised in petty detail ever since. Probable cause becomes a whim, and privacy a form of obstructing justice.

In modern society, political heresy is more dangerous than religious heresy. But against that risk, the Manual offers three political objects for the dog soldier, defend freedom, accept law, and project your belief in freedom and justice into the circles of your kinship by example and deed.

The very idea of the dog soldier is a product of the intensely free and individualistic tribal culture. When the dog soldier stakes himself to the ground to thwart the advance of the enemy, the point is not to achieve heroic proportions, but to protect and preserve the people, their freedom and their independence, from depredations, destruction, and slavery. Defend freedom, fight injustice, and protect the people from the enemies that would prey upon them.

In modern society, knowing where the enemy is advancing is not very clear, but the threat is constant and very real. Jefferson believed in generational revolutions, around every twenty years or so, not as some irrational Maoist edict, but because he saw that power, no matter how slight, will organize and fix everything it can. Unless each generation saw for itself the great virtues and benefits of freedom, even tasting what is means to fight for them, the Great American Experiment would wind down, whimper, and fail like the Ancient Greeks and the Romans, unable to handle its complexities of social organization, and like the Republic, cast away the tribal liberties it sought to incorporate into governance, and adopt the totalitarian approach of empire. In the end, just another empire on history's landscapes, the heresy of human freedom snuffed out again, until, one can hope, it breaks out again some day in the future. The dog soldier's mission is to keep the flame of liberty alive.

Still, the alternative of anarchy and mob rule is unacceptable. When all order breaks down, monstrous acts occur, as has happened in recent times in South Central Los Angeles, the Balkan states, and the islands of Indonesia. Destroying the basis of social organization makes social survival a primitive, wasteful happenstance again. Even if committed to the minimalist tribal view of government, some governance of the people is necessary for them to stay a people. Render unto Caesar what is Caesar's. You cannot change or overthrow the government by cheating it or picking fights with it. You change government by changing the people. Speak in praise of human freedom, and act with honor, and people will see that such beliefs and conduct make a good person. Resent and resist the loss of rights and freedoms, for yourself and for others, endure government, and exercise your free speech, your right to associate, and the attractive power of noble conduct and just deeds to change the culture. If Jefferson's notions of generational political revolutions were successfully carried out as cultural revolutions in outbreaks of freedom, liberty, and justice, the government, as long as it is by the people, will gradually evolve and change. One can hope intelligence finally shows up.

In the end, the dog soldier must be proactive in defense of freedom. It is not enough to treasure the flames of liberty, or endure the impersonal obfuscation of domineering bureaucracies. There is work that can be done today. The true goal is not government, but sensible social organization.

This is the final political object for the dog soldier, to re-establish with the modern, dispersed society, the tribal instincts of kinship in the people that are stable, reciprocal, economically viable, mutually reinforcing, and culturally survivable.

The pristine world of the tribe is gone. The great herds of mammoths and bison are gone. The conditions of our past origins cannot be recovered, nor do we want their return. If the heresy of human freedom is to survive, it must do so in modern social reality. The dog soldier's faith is simple. Trust the hundred thousand years of human conditioning. Make the pride and the tribal sized group work. This is to work at the very roots of social organization, what we call the grassroots, where the effect is the most genuine, where it counts the most, human to human. Be just here, and a just society is possible.

Cultural Competence

A people's culture is all their learned ways of doing things, loosely called their customs, practices, rituals, rites,

mores, and etiquettes. Culture covers everything from how to talk in various circumstances, how to dress accordingly, how to grieve, marry, and raise children, to all the little technologies people employ to get about their living, like tying shoes, driving cars, using checking accounts, and cooking food. All mixed up in this functional stuff are amusements, aesthetics, celebrations, music, myths, dance, and lore.

At the tribal level, the business of acquiring the customary practices and common skills that make up cultural competence is relatively uniform. The package each adult possesses is largely the same as that possessed by other adults. Some subgroups and subcultures today achieve this uniformity. But in modern society, with its vast populations, cities, and its condition of dispersal, fluent cultural competence is much more complicated and fragmented. Numerous, diverse subcultures appear, based on ethnic heritage, regional isolation, or common lifestyle, often juxtaposed and seldom amalgamated, each as different in its ways as any primal tribe. To counterbalance all these centrifugal forces, modern society attempts popular culture. The people overall must have something in common, no matter how inherently shallow or manufactured the phenomena.

One ends up with a remarkable cultural panorama where many adults among the people share only some of the same cultural package. Most of us end up cultural mulattos. What we have as cultural competence proves a composite of ways drawn from any number of subcultures mixed with whatever aspects of popular culture that captures our fancy. This is the true boon of diversity in a culture of freedom, not in the museum like preservation of endangered cultural species, but in the infusion of new ways, through personal choice, preference, and invention, into the cultural competence of any free adult ranging across the greater people.

The challenge of cultural competence in modern society confronts the dog soldier with two complementing objects. First, consciously develop as broad a based cultural competence as individually possible. Plunder all the sources of cultural diversity and build up your cultural prowess as suits your tastes, needs, and wants. In order to come from the people, one must be comfortable among them. Know their history, understand their ways, their customs and celebrations, and master their technologies. You cannot be dog soldier and live apart or insulated from the people.

Second, practice the Golden Rule of Tolerance, "Live and Let Live". Achieving cultural competence does not require slavish conformity to custom and convention, nor blind, uncritical acceptance of everything the culture presents. But neither can you find all in contempt. A free culture will allow each individual to choose what features of culture they will relate to. Find yours. And see that others, in their own way, are seeking the same.

An excellent illustration of the value of measured tolerance is found in the American passion for sports teams, for tradeoffs between the good and the bad are clearly evident. On the downside, picking fights with rival fans and burning down whole city blocks in celebration of winning the ultimate championship is a sorry reminder of human imperfection. Not unlike the end of Imperial Constantinople, where the city descended first into civil war, then into anarchy, the competing factions manned by the fans of the traditional rival charioteer teams, the Reds, Greens, Blues and Yellows. The color of your jacket meant friend, foe or death, for no rational reason.

But for many of the people, the sports teams are a way of uniting themselves with each other, something to have in common with others that they can talk about and identify with, something besides the weather. When they root and cheer, they express and satisfy the deep human need to be emotionally involved with a tribe, sharing its successes and failures alike. One may eschew the game, decry the excesses, but still see the powerful and underlying good effects of the contests on the health of the people, especially when in the modern condition of kinship dispersal. It does no harm to others, and much good to those who play.

Ideally, the dog soldier is the universal, native stranger, able to move easily among the people they meet, old or new, able to identify with and move into comfortable, personal relation with any of the kinship well met and well known. You cannot use the discouraging conditions of modern society to become more alien to most you encounter. The confoundedness of modern society only makes the appearance of the dog soldier all the more important to the people. There are already too many enemy strangers walking the strange land. How can you protect, defend, and elevate the people if you cannot belong to them and be happy among them? Person to person commerce transcends cultural trappings. Adapt personally to the person you are with. Enjoy their apparent cultural differences without petty criticisms.

Above all, see that the combination of a culture of freedom and cultural diversity creates a marvelous milieu in which to refine your personal package of cultural competence, your own ways of doing things. When you find something that makes effective sense to you, try it, and if it helps, adopt it. Cultural practices in a culture of freedom are like trade goods in a free market. What proves suitable or effective spreads by force of real value.

Possessions

Apart from their ranges and territories, and what they soon intend to eat, animals are possessed only of themselves. Humans are unique among the animal kingdom in that they not only form the idea of having things, they form tight psychological attachments to the things so possessed. In extreme, this bond becomes greed, a need and craving to possess more. Humans not only become attached to the material objects they possess, but they will go to considerable lengths to hold onto their possessions, building bigger closets to store the stuff, even burying their property in their graves to insure that what they have they will keep, even into the next world.

One reason humans are so materially possessive is because material things, especially tools, make a serious difference in how we live. If possessed only of ourselves as are the animals, we would have to live like the animals. We have been able to do much better than that from the beginning. Humans make things out of the environment that significantly improve our material well being, making it more pleasant, comfortable, productive, and healthier. Part of what make us human is how we create and employ a material mileau around us to our advantage.

But with possessions and property comes the damnable problem of to have and to have not, that is, how is the wealth to be distributed among the people. Inequality in material possession is an inevitable feature of all human society, tribal or modern. But at the tribal level, several factors operate to keep the wealth normally distributed, that is, in the classic fat, bell curve. First, the ranges of actual wealth discrepancies are small. Second, the possessions of all are open to public inspection. Any can see how much or how little one has. Some inequality is tolerable, especially if most individuals are near the middling average. But outlandish differences suffer social disapprobation, and tend to correct themselves through kinship dynamics. Third, the reciprocity of kinship also works to keep the extremes from becoming dysfunctional. The well to do are expected to give away surplus wealth in some fashion to the less possessed. Among the Pacific Northwest Indians, this leveling is achieved through the potlatch. Each year, the greatest chief in the tribe is the one who gives away the most through potlatch feasts and festivities.

For a tribe to survive and succeed, all its members must succeed. All must be counted upon to cooperate and work together as a whole. This is the whole point of kinship across the tribe, to keep the whole first and foremost in the minds of all. Severe material disparities sow discord and envy among all sentient humans. Kinship breaks down, and the people fragment. Even a cow can see the greener grass and resents the fence.

In modern society, none of these constraining influences operate to naturally encourage a normal, fat in the middle, distribution of the wealth. First, the ranges of wealth are enormous, and by the rules of the modern monopoly game, a few may come into possession of nearly all the wealth. Second, while there is a great deal of public viewing of horded wealth, those that are allowed to get up close for a detailed inspection are individuals who have only slightly less wealth than the exhibitor. The rest of us see the mansions from afar. Nor do the rich in modern society have to walk past the dwellings of the modest and the poor, and really see how they live a day in the life. Were the rich and the poor bound in kinship, and allowed and expected to visit each other's domiciles, the fantastic extremes modern society condones in its skewed, impersonal distribution of the wealth would soon regress back toward the mean and fatten the middle of the healthier bell curve.

Third, there is no compunction of reciprocity in the modern world. Remarkably, a fair number of the contemporary rich give away large sums freely, as if competing in a potlatch, but most of that goes into foundations and the pockets of bureaucrats, and not into the hands of individuals. Few actually test the Gospels and give directly to the poor all wealth beyond their personal needs without expectation or presumed subservience.

In modern society, the citizen is expected to spend their way up into higher and higher standards of living, devoting their increases in wealth to conspicuous consumption that displays the true emerging status and superior social standing. Were there some intelligible limit to individual wealth, this game would finally reach some end point, beyond which new increases are superfluous, and are recycled back into the kinship and the people in simple acts of generosity.

The Manual offers a handful of objects concerning possessions for the working dog soldier. All follow from the idea of keeping the business simple.

Sensibly secure what possessions you need. The rewards and graces of ample material living are not to be eschewed. There is no necessary dog soldier vow of poverty. Have what you need. Know that more is luxury. If you win luxury, enjoy it, share it. But do not give in and need it.

Take care of what you do have. Once the material merit of a man was judged by how well they took care of what possessions they had, be they few or many, modest or impressive. If you cannot keep what you have in repair and presentable, maybe you have too much. If you do not know how much or what you have, you do have too much.

Limit your emotional attachment to the items of your property to a sentimental few. Some possessions are to be cherished, but most are just things. There should be no undue grief at their loss, or a driving fixation in their gain.

Study and perfect the saddle bag set of your possessions, that precise personal set that one takes along on travels. On the Western frontier, it was observed that the man who could travel light, yet effectively, was the one free to move readily and immediately into the new opening lands of opportunity. Travel possessions should be spare, spartan, but complete. When you strip yourself down from time to time, you free yourself for greater ranges of action and endeavor. Mobility is a great asset, a great maker of experience.

Finally, develop and keep a clear idea of just how much you really need to live comfortably enough and fully enough to suit yourself. When you secure this, what more you enjoy as increases in wealth is simply serendipity. Pass the serendipity along. Be creative in your generosity. Test the Gospels, and give without worry of return. If you have so many possessions that you cannot remember all of what you have, you have too many possessions and should give some away.

It is said that you cannot take it with you. Death allows not even our material body. But how you live your life, the good you do, the moral victories you win, these become one with your soul, and go with you. They are you. The greatest riches are the ones that go with us in the crossover.

Manners

Good manners are the mark of decency. They are the nurturing fabric of positive social exchange at its most intimate level, face to face, eye to eye. First and last, our manner is what others see and feel when being with us, or dealing with us. Do we come across warm, open and considerate, or do we come across stiff, overbearing, surly, and put out at the bother of having to have manners at all? Do you like being with people, or is it a chore? Your manners will reveal this difference.

The manners sought are not the polite and petty forms of etiquette, to often combined with the European Social Disease to beg superior status. Rather they are to be found in the deeper origins and motivations of all behavior toward others. Etiquette is matter of conformity, manners that of genuineness. True manners are not rote, memorized behaviors displayed on cue, but are the spontaneous expressions of a generous spirit guided by deeper moral precepts.

Good manners are easy manners, the kind that can pick up and play in a natural way wherever people gather in a friendly, talkative way. Good manners are good company wherever they are. Good manners are also comfortable manners. They set others at ease, and in return, yourself. Finally, good manners are creative manners. They fit the occasion, even heighten it. They can make the most mundane of encounters memorable.

Good manners and the graceful refinements of comportment arise from three basic relationships with your fellow human being, understanding them, respecting them, and enjoying them.

Teach yourself to observe others. Know people as the human animals they really are. Understand in them what you understand in yourself. Understanding how others are to be approached and regarded should have everything to do with how you would want to be approached and regarded. Study the characteristics ways of people, and choose among your repertoire of manners, those ways that complement theirs. The dog soldier's goal is be at home with any and all of the people that fate throws us into and among. Good manners are like a shared warm blanket. They make us common to each other instead of separating, or worse, alienating, ourselves from each other.

The deepest source of good manners is respect for the rights of others and their essential human dignity. Whatever rights and freedoms you grant yourself, unless you grant them equally to all others, your claims are without merit. The Golden Rule has been phrased many ways but has not been improved.

The true expression of respect is a moving thing, flowing from you to others who unerringly feel and appreciate the real thing. To be kind is a great ability, especially to women, children, the elderly and the helpless. You embrace their dignity and give it back to them. They return the genuineness, and this, you will find, feels good, real good.

A commitment to good manners and the wisdom that underwrites them, however, does not oblige you to suffer fools, indulge the obnoxious, or endure the company of idiots. Neither does rude behavior need to be tolerated. There are ways those strong in presence can call a pig, "a pig", and subject them to the public inspection of those around, without sinking to their level.

"Civilized" society spawns miscreants and they will be encountered more often than wished. But the sad contrast they provide can become one of your most powerful motives to express finer conduct. Look at them and see for yourself how you would never allow yourself to behave or act like that. Chances then are that you won't. Then see to it that your dealings with miscreant come to an end. One lesson should be enough for a dog soldier.

In general, treat others in a decent, friendly way. Be courteous and civil, and above all, be kind. Know and understand how contagious one good word or deed can be, for one good word can change the life of the one to whom we offer it. Though we seldom see its spreading ranges, the kindness done to one, becomes a kindness passed along in new forms to many others. Only some modern humans are toads and ingrates.

Be governed by genuineness and the truth in your dealings with others, and your dealings will be fair and pleasant. Smile and share humor. Give encouragement to others whenever you can. It is the finest thing we do for each other. Enjoy others and they will instinctively enjoy us back.

Conduct

When our actions are guided by the ideals and principles we call virtues, we elevate the human condition, in ourselves and for others. This inner guidance of conduct is the work of character, those virtues we have engrained in ourselves, our manifest sense of honor. Without ideals or principles truly affecting one's conduct, one merely behaves, an ordinary dog or a drone.

You will know the dog soldier by their good works. Virtue for virtue's sake is not the main point of honor. While honor may be personal, its play is social. Unless our conduct has an impact on the lives of others for the better, honor is sterile and vain. A true sense of honor is dynamic. It seeks its applications. Through the instrument of principled conduct, something good is created in the kinship and the people. Whether a problem is solved, or a kind word given, some work is performed that increases the total good in the universe that much more.

Too often, however, adherence to ideals and principles is judged in terms of conformity to orthodox forms, the words easy to recite by rote and motions easy to go through. Conduct is not simple. Conduct must be driven by goals and objects, and judged by its effects, not by the correct imitation of contrived conformities. To dare true conduct is to face risk. That is where the honor comes from.

Conduct begins by consciously choosing to have a sense of honor, and then in carrying out one's life in new ways in the struggle to fulfill the teachings of that sense. Conduct is an ongoing process of self betterment, expressed and tested in the public forum. We can, through review and reflection, study and judge our actions, their motives and their consequences. We can see our shortcomings and resolve to do better. Conduct is a matter of finding and expressing what we find best in ourselves and giving it to others. Conduct reveals how we view ourselves, and the character we are becoming.

Walk among the people, liking them and enjoying their distinctive natures. Do not expect beautiful people or angels, nor demons and villains. Just expect the people to be human, maddening sometimes, but admirable as often. Recognize and hail their good moments, feel for them in their bad ones, and brace them with the truth of their misconduct, firmly and caring at once, for they are the people. We must live amongst each other. This should be both enjoyable and uplifting. When they succeed, we succeed.

Remember that you are human, too. You have your own limits and imperfections. A commitment to a life of good works does not mean that you must be superman, your strength and goodwill inexhaustible. It is not a point of honor to allow yourself to be taken advantage of, again and again. Most good works will involve you in other people's problems. These, its seems, are inexhaustible, and can drag even a Samson down.

The dog soldier must be sensible and selective in what they can take on and actually deliver upon. The works of conduct should show up all through the social ranges, from the inner circles of the kinship to the everyday, common stranger. But the concentration of works within the kinship is what makes the kinship work. To be selective is human, and a recognition of our limits and our rights to set priorities.

In concluding these matters of conduct, a warning is necessary. If you pursue a dynamic course of conduct, and defend and aid others, you will raise up enemies, no matter how well meaning or good your intentions. The position of the Manual is to set up no one as your enemy. The hope of kinship is that all will be on the same side. But expect that someone else will likely set up you up as an enemy, whether you are aware of this malignance or not. Through jealously, harbored grudges, Freudian demons, or just plain meanness, some will actively seek to bring about your downfall in harm or misfortune, usually through calumnies and cabals hidden from your sight. You do have to see who is acting as your enemy when they appear. You have to know the real threats. You have to expect to be blooded.

You have a right to self defense. But the best strategy is usually to get out of harm's way, and failing that, pursue your own integrity. Direct defense may be justified, sometimes unavoidable, but it is also the dogrope. Expect to go out with the enemy.

A broader defense to evil and its petty incarnations is needed. The people never have too many dog soldiers. You can do something about that. Bring out the soldier in those around you. Reinforce honor in others. When you see good ideas, recognize them. When you see worthy goals, commend them. When you see sound maneuvers, point them out. When you see decent conduct, praise it. Do this at all times possible, selflessly, free of envy or petty criticism, with all the genuineness your personal presence commands.

Raise up and encourage the dog soldier in others. When you tell people that they have done a good thing, they internalize that conduct just a little more, making themselves more prone to better deeds to come. When you believe that someone can be great, sometimes they prove you right. The miscreant and the malformed will always prey upon the weak. One great way to protect the weak is to make them strong. Build up others in the ways of good works, and the enemies of kinship are that much more on the run.

Fortune and Failure

Good things happen. Bad things happen. Sometimes the fate of nations is at stake, sometimes merely personal inconvenience. Sometimes we are part responsible, but often we are not. We call it luck because no man can cause it.

Most human cultures develop some approach to the vagaries of fortune. Some read stars or pigeon livers. Some ingest psychotropic substances to fire visions of the future. Some school shamans or prophets to foretell what is to come. All seek to gain some edge on fortune. None have ever succeeded better than a coin toss over the true run of history.

Fortune comes upon us two ways. First, we are born into a world already shaped by fortune. We may be to the manner born or not. We get the genetic package our parents bequeath us without mercy. And we get them as parents and the way they will raise us without appeal. Personal choice, merit, and preferences have nothing to do with these matters. We just get them. They are the shape of our origins, the nature and the breeding with which we all begin. Through disciplines, we can mold ourselves into new beings, but we must do so from the roots fortune has provided. Pretending otherwise usually impairs the process of true self growth. What we can become is vastly more important than what we are natively. But you cannot become anything without starting with what you are. That is fortune's play, not yours.

But fortune also breaks day to day. Coincidental events strike in strange ways. Sometimes we are the right place and the right time. Sometimes it all goes wrong despite our best efforts. Sometimes you find a five dollar bill. Sometimes you lose one.

In both ways, in starting position and breaking reality, fortune sets the challenges and adversities that make up real human life. In this sense, the dog soldier is the true soldier of fortune. Where fortune challenges or threatens, there the dog soldier is needed. For challenge can be met, and adversity overcome. But not all are equally suited to do so. Another curse of fortune. But where one may be defeated, two may rally, recover lost ground, and advance. Sometimes the good fortune itself is the appearance of the dog soldier, ready to join forces and make things go better for the good of the people.

But you may also be flat out defeated. Strive and you always risk failure. To be human is to dwell in imperfection and disappointment. We have failings, shortcomings, and just plain outrageous bad luck. There is no striving without also running the risk of failure, in the eyes of others, or in one's own eyes. Failure happens and happens often, sometimes in grand ways, sometimes in subtle, almost unnoticed ways. Failure is a basic playing condition in human life.

There is only one healthy response to failure, and that is to take it, and then to get back up and try again. Study failure, see the truth of its causes, in yourself, in others, and in the situation which did you in. Much of what is called failure is a relative phenomena anyway. Indeed, the insightful often see the seeds of new opportunities in every failing circumstance, making it merely a passing phase in one's progressive destiny. Many of history's most renowned successes sprang from individuals well experienced in failure. Many a good saint was once a great sinner.

It is a hard counsel that recommends courting failure, but without facing challenge and adversity, the deeper foundations of character are unattainable. The only true failure is internal, when one quits and gives up inside. Once this happens consistently, one neither succeeds or fails. They are simply moved about by fate, devoid of will, mere drones in a system they pray will continue to reward their conformities.

Personal Legend

When we are gone, disappearing from this life as we will, we are remembered by those who must remain behind. Our manners, presence, and conduct can set deeply in the memory of others. This is legend, and exists apart from us, in the minds of all those we touched in our living days. You do not have to be heroic or celebrated, the legend is still there in the tracks of your life on the living.

But the creation of legend, that is the work of this lifetime. Look upon it as the artwork of honor, and participate in the process. In the making of personal legend, a man defines himself by marking the defining moments that made him. A man has a right to celebrate his achievements in character, his feats and accomplishments, and his pursuit of honor. The expression of this originality as a whole is one's personal legend which includes one's manners, style, appearance, and personal aesthetics. It includes how we are known to others, and also includes those things that may be known only to God and us. That would be enough for a dog soldier.

A life of choices in a culture of conformity breeds stale drones out of otherwise sound human male stock. A life of choices in a culture of freedom makes original individuals. This will be manifest in personal legend, the characteristic ways, habits, penchants, and appearances that make up and give substance to the original identity. The dog soldier knows who they are and how they are, and will express this creatively in personal myths, totems, emblems, decor, ornamentation, and tall tales.

Legend is created out of the stuff of one's life and its significant experiences, and becomes the record of what you have become. This is a creative enterprise to be enjoyed, and becomes the basis for remembering who you are. To be born human is to be born with original nature, both as a species and as an individual. Understanding who we are, displaying it with a personal, creative touch, and carrying it forward with us through our lives, is to recognize that life is a cumulative process of identity, cultivated and refined by age and experience, a result to be celebrated, as much for ourselves as for others. Our efforts add color to the lives of others and ourselves. Through personal legend, our manner, our preferences, our adornments, and the story of our personal history, we reinforce who we are. We consummate our originality as free human beings.

DESIDERATA

In Praise of Human Freedom

If there were no true freedom to defend, no dog soldiers would rise up to defend it. Only drones would be available to play soldier. Living human freedom intensely makes a strong people. No greater honor, no greater contribution, is possible beyond placing one's mortality on the line to protect and defend the people, the kinship of your world and life.

The culture of freedom can lead to harmony, happiness and fulfillment in the kinship. But only if it comes with challenge. The Cheyenne and the American Pioneer found freedom by moving westward into the frontier. No one around to tell them how to live, what to do, how to talk and how to think. Free to live their lives on the terms they chose and set for themselves, to the extent to which their ability allowed. If they could defend it and keep it.

The Indian and the Pioneer also found uncertainty, danger, and adversity. To survive and succeed they needed to learn and develop new ways of living, materially, socially and personally. When you succeed under frontier conditions, your sense of freedom and independence is permanently stamped into your originality and your character. You can abide no other way. Freedom becomes something you cannot live without. Something you fight to keep, as fiercely as humanly possible, something you cannot surrender without dying inside even if you still live biologically. If you cannot reach the point of "live free or die", you never were really free to begin with.

Genuine freedom, lived fully, makes a healthier individual, mentally, morally, and physically. It fosters an emotional life more truly satisfying than what wealth, power, or status, can ever concoct. It opens the space needed for the fulfillment of the great human potential, and makes a strong, vibrant, and resilient people, a kinship that can endure and prosper.

But freedom is easily lost. It can be taken by enemies who conquer, exploit, plunder and subjugate, in big pieces or little pieces, in one fell swoop or by steadily chipping away. Freedom can be lost from outside of society, or bartered away from the inside. The ever pretending ruling class is ever in favor of rigid organization and enforced conformity. Anything to keep things from ever changing. The status quo is their privilege and security. Freedom is also easily sold out by the individual themselves, in exchange for money, status, security, and derivative power. If one can sell out one's soul to the Devil, selling out your freedom is a relatively easy task.

Securing and keeping a true and full ranging freedom is seldom easy. The challenge comes with the territory. To be real, freedom must be seen, pursued, earned, enjoyed and defended. The demands of the defense of freedom is a task for all, but among the people, it falls most heavily upon the male. Larger, more reliably mobile, and not biologically capable of carrying, bearing, and nurturing the newborn, the male must grow to be a man, and more, must learn to become dog soldier.

Perhaps women are more blessed in making a beautiful, satisfying society, but it be the dog soldiers who protect and keep it so.

THE RIGHT TO BE A MAN

The greatest drawback in advocating positive male culture is the fact that so many boorish and cretin societies throughout recent human history have been male dominated or patriarchal. But in the first ten thousand years of tribal village and farming society, the sexes were equally valued, involved, and empowered in setting and effecting the course and progress of the people. There are no signs of fortification, no lost weapons, no evidence of pillage, destruction or massacre. The technologies that could produce surplus males in abundance and the food supply necessary to feed the armies they would become took a long time coming.

But once these armies appeared, as with the Kurgans of the Russian Steppes and Sargon I in Mesopotamia, conquest, confiscation, coercion, and wide scale physical and psychological terror became possible. War became an institution. These were the first "civilizations" and so called empires, built on conquest and all privilege to the victor. For the vanquished, true freedom was lost. They became the lower class and disappear from history.

The European Social Disease has had long precedence. "Civilized" societies, formed by physical might and maintained through the repressive police powers of the State, carefully articulate, follow, and enforce hierarchies of domination, lords over vassals, husbands over wives, citizens over slaves. The presuming ruling class sells the Big Lie and makes the people eat it.

The Cheyenne did not abuse their women, either physically or psychologically, except without bringing shame down upon themselves and their name. They were shocked and repelled by the liberty with which white men vigorously and without shame beat their women and children. Like the Iroquois, the female lineage structured society. The shame and low esteem of the women was the greatest shame of all. It was easier for a

161

woman to divorce a man, then for a man to do the same. The lodge and its property belonged to her. Divorced males were lucky to find a place in the dog soldier's lodge, once they came in from the cold from living in the bushes like dogs, so great was their shame.

The women kept the lodge, the home, the heart of the people. If they failed, there was little point in having warriors. The people were lost and doomed as surely if they had been conquered and subjugated by aliens. But in reality, most contested tribal ranges were composed of relatively even tribes. Each tribe, even the marginal ones, had enough warriors, men strong enough to be brave and able in defending and securing the people's survival. The tribes would fight fiercely to drive and keep away threatening enemy tribes. But if they stayed away, or made peace, that was the end of it. Total conquest, domination and mass enslavement did not happen. The American Indian had to catch the European Social Disease much like they did small pox and cholera, from the Europeans and their descendants.

A horrid rumor in the nightmare of politically correct insanity has it that feminists in Norway are undertaking a program, beginning at birth and including castration, to condition young boys to grow up to be like women. To rid the world of wicked male aggression. Perhaps this is a logical response by women, even if half witted, to a modern male culture that has gone bizerk and limp at the same time. A more aggressive action is hard to imagine. The only serious improvement to insuring such an end would be to surgically castrate all little boys in the fourth month of pregancy before any squirt of tetesterone can corrupt their femininity.

We are born male and female, the choice made for us biologically. The natural truth cannot be evaded. The female carries, bears, and keeps alive the newborn, the future of the people. The male, mostly by default, must see that this happens, in defense of which their life must be readily given.

First there is the people, the kinship. To keep and sustain them, the whole, both male and female are needed. Neither is more or less because nature has made the sexes different, with each suited for the roles the other is not. Both differences are necessary and work quite well and effectively together in their complimentary interplay.

The recognition of this natural truth does not imply that men should be all masculine, and women all feminine. First we are human, the rest is detail. The same wonderful human ability and potential courses through all of us, male and female alike. We are far more alike then we might like to believe, despite all the dimorphism of our bodies and biologies. There is a feminine side to men, and a masculine side to women. Each sex should seek and develop their opposite sides. This makes strong and balanced men and women, what the people need most. Women who get men to fix their cars and solve their problems by flaunting the liberties we grant them in displaying and highlighting their sexual attributes are just as imbalanced and defective as mortician suited men who presume that all women should "mommy" them.

The basic truth remains, men are equipped in biologically different ways from women, placing them in roles that match that natural difference, just as women are. These tribal cultural roles have had 30,000 years of natural selection to reinforce them.

All men have a right to discover, explore, and develop that different potential that comes from being born male.

CONCERNING WOMEN

No apologies. The Manual is a work in male culture. This is no knock on women as warriors. Open always to the truth of things, the Cheyenne revered the courageous feats of their women. Great respect was given to Buffalo Road Woman for saving her brother at the Battle of the Rosebud, a week before Custer's Last Stand. Under heavy fire and far from friendly lines, she rescued her wounded brother from abandonment before the withering fire of the bluecoats. The Cheyenne named the battle after her deed. She was their MVP, Most Valuable Player.

To the Cheyenne, the women were the most precious resource of the people, and the bellweather of their destiny. It was said that as long as the women were strong and had hope, the people would survive, no matter how hard bad fortune fell. But if the women lost heart, no amount of bravery by men could save the people.

The female warrior was also an accepted tradition of the Celts, another restless, westward moving people, also prizing deeply, freedom and the original individual. When the people are threatened, all able bodies are welcome on the front line. But no sane people would put the majority of their strong, young women at peril of maiming or death, for this would surely doom any people to lingering extinction.

Neither can the hard reality of nature be safely ignored. No amount of pluck will save a well endowed female, five foot two, against a Chicago Bear linebacker. Nature has given the birth and nurturing of the infant to the female, and thrust the larger male into the role of defense and protection, even to the point of violent combat.

On the other hand, there is nothing in the Manual that pertains exclusively to men. Its underwriting paradigm is human, essentially indifferent to gender. There is no human female that is somehow inherently incapable of the character this Manual defines. Indeed, the more true dog soldiers found in modern humanity, the better off we all are. The Celt and the Cheyenne understood this. But they were also sane. The purpose of the dog soldier is to defend and protect the women, the children, the old, and the helpless, so that the women are free to fulfill their own purpose, to raise and keep the people. If the women are not strong, no greatness by men matters.

A sane, natural understanding like that of the Celts and the Cheyenne, one would think, ought to be universal. But the human brain is far from adequate in defeating the twists and abscesses of peculiar "civilized" practices. The Moche on the West coast of Peru, irrigated the desert with the waters of the far distant Andes. But in the face of persistent El Ninos that turned their land into a vicious, rapid sliding, eroding mud slope, they sacrificed nearly all of their next generation, both male and female, though virgin girls are always a sacrificial specialty. When the devastating rains and quakes stopped, there were too few Moche left strong enough to rebuild. Miscreant insanity comes with the gift of humanity.

In diversified, amalgamated, interspersed modern society, such collective malfunctions do not occur on such a major scale. Rather, little pockets of humanity cross over into delusion, like Jim Jones and his cult's mass suicide in Guyana. The greater problem is the aberration of individual human males into creatures who cause more harm, distress, misery, and sadness among the people than any good that "civilization" might attach to their existance could ever outweigh.. These are the malformed, the miscreant, and without close involvement with tribal culture and its goals of honor and greatness, these human orcs, these misbegotten mockeries of the finer human potential, flourish. The people never have too many dog soldiers.

A Strong and Vibrant People

Being bred to and practicing the ways of the dog soldier is not merely a personal phenomena. It comes with a full package of social benefits. The life of the dog soldier increases the general good in society, by upholding truth, by helping the needy, by being strong when called upon, and by fighting injustice and defending the ways of freedom. Through example and deed, the dog soldier affects all society.

Expect the people to be human. They will be imperfect, limited, sometimes good and great, sometimes mean and unkind. But remember they are us. You make a difference. The balance between a strong, heathy people and a hive of queens and drones can be slender. Sometimes the long odds are hopeless, like William Wallace. But the fight is between being human and alive, and the fate of robots and insects.

The dog soldier lives and walks among the people, knowing them and uplifting them, without needing outright reward, praise or favors in consideration. There is nothing wrong with material reward and social recognition. If they happen, fine. If not, so what? Nor does the mission require the dog soldier to be a gullible fool, to be promiscuously taken advantage of. Rather, it is the knowledge of one's true impact, something that cannot be taken away, that is the real reward. Good dog soldiers tip the balance in favor of the culture of freedom, and make strong people, a people resilient, indomitable, happy and satisfied. A people fulfilling the finest of human potential in the bosom of freedom. The people never have too many dog soldiers.

For one who truly lives freedom, fighting to keep one's freedom, defending it beyond reason, is not patriotic hype, a bunch of slogans to chant while going into combat. Once bred to freedom, one possesses an instinct that cannot be compromised. If confined in a culture of conformity, one finds that they might as well be dead. People with very little freedom will not fight very hard to keep what little they have. People with an extremely powerful sense of freedom are extremely hard to kill.

To become original Cheyenne or American, human nature is put to the test. The conditions of freedom and independence are essentially conditions of challenge and adversity. One either charges forward when faced with freedom and all its proving trails, and becomes original and self reliant, or one falls back into the past and its convenient orthodox programming, conforming anxiously to the contrived mores and attitudes of stereotyping, mousetrap minds, a puppet of the self righteous and the presuming ruling class, and a slave to lies they dain to feed you.

The Dog Soldier's Pride

The most telling modern condition for all, the kinship, the enemy, and the dog soldier, is geographical dispersal. The tight, reassuring contiguity of archaic tribal life is gone. The only intelligent recourse is to deal with this as simply another playing condition, and adapt, keeping true to the essential qualities of kinship and honor.

The dog soldier will often appear alone, rogue, not fully knowing what they are becoming, or have become. But over time, others will be met, and a pride will be shared for knowing who and what each really are, a shared pride earned by crossing the rivers of life together.

In a modern culture of freedom, this will be a free forming process, hit and miss, and even when attained, suffering from risk of new dispersals. The faith must be that once well known and bonded is always well known and bonded, even if the tides of personal destiny separate each for the rest of the lifetime.

Only very rare individuals can survive the wilderness, frontier or modern, wholy alone. Isolation is usually only a sorry, perhaps pathetic, life and fate. The natural tendency of the dog soldiers will be to band together in groups large enough to be survivable. Groupings up to the size of the Lion's Pride, eight to fifteen, about the number of lodges in a Cheyenne band, will work.

Were society to breakdown, the Dark Ages to be revisited, the dog soldier pride will be the last defense against anarchy. And the survivable, enduring unit upon which society may be rebuilt.

The Carbon in the Steel

We can envy the dog its unshakeable loyalty. The dog need have no other purpose than to just be with you, wherever you are, whatever you are doing. It might look at you strangely if it is out in the rain that you choose, but the dog will be there beside you until you decide enough of the nonsense. The human has the same pack animal breeding as the dog, and the same natural capacity of loyalty, but the fulfillment of loyalty in the human is far from reliable. A man can feign loyalty, keeping his true loyalties hidden. Or a man can deny the obligation and rationalize away the washing of the hands. Finally, any man can set themselves apart and think only of their personal self, first and last. Human trust and loyalty is a risky business. Human loyalties are hard earned, hard won, and still they are terribly perishable.

A man's loyalties are his life. They are his reasons and motives for living. The loyalties we keep or abandon define us in the eyes of others. If we are honest, they define us in our own eyes. We are all aware of the acts of betrayal, or the acts of affirmation, that we make. More importantly, though, our loyalties define how we are to be counted upon. Fairweather friends and sunshine patriots may be good company at parties, but loyal friends are the only ones you count on riding the river with. They stay the course, rain or hail. In what ways can you be counted upon?

You cannot keep any virtue, or fulfill any ideal, if you cannot stay loyal to the obligations in conduct and presence those virtues and ideals demand of you. Loyalties are the footings of our character. Their strength is measured in years. You cannot give one up and simply replace it, anymore than you can pour a hundred year bottle of wine down the sink and replace it overnight. You have to wait another hundred years.

Loyalty and its affirmations are the carry through in our growing. They bring the foundations of past choice and practice forward into the present, and project us into the future, a little stronger, a little deeper, as we experience the surges and windshears of responsibility and response that come with every a new day of living. What we remain loyal to, these are the deepest roots of our maturation. The longer they sink in and set, the higher we can stand.

Add carbon to iron, and what is strong suddenly becomes stronger and more resilient. Our conscious choice of virtues and ideals are the iron in our inner makeup. Our loyalty to those virtues and ideals is the carbon which makes the steel of real character, giving it a lasting endurance far beyond its first measure.

Like the carbon in the steel, loyalites brace us for our severest test of character, those occasions where it is easy to to give a blind eye and turn away. There are plenty of socially sanctioned rationalizations available to excuse our negligence or apathy. We can turn into insects and just buzz off. Loyalty shows itself when conduct in inconvenient. We hold true to what we believe ourselves to be, through hard times, bad times, and hopeless times. There are always reasons to break away and disengage. Always our personal selves that we can place first and foremost in any matter. Loyalty is what makes us stay with things, be they ideals, people, or beliefs. The affirmations of loyalty are the well springs of our pride, our dignity, and our self esteem. When we fail loyalty, we lose a lot, a terrible lot.

When true loyalty is genuinely shared among people, a wonderful thing happens. The seeds of kinship germinate and grow. In the modern world of dispersal, this is a great achievement. If the people cannot be loyal to each other, a just society is not possible. In fact, without widespread loyalty among the people, society is not possible. What you get is like what you have when you remove the trees from the forest, a lumber yard of cleanly shaved deadwood.

The Miscreant and the Malformed

It was said among the Cheyenne that some men just live. To become dog soldier was to rise above the common, the baseline. But the Cheyenne were a noble people. Their mediocre were still of the people, belonged to the people, and made their contribution to provide for the success of the whole. The Law of Kinship governed. There was a responsibility to all by all.

Among the modern human, this clear loyalty is easily and often lost, turned queer, and the male so twisted, becomes alien to the people, any people save themselves. This is the new enemy, the scoundrel sharks and their organized gangs that prey upon those that belong to your people.

In the tribal world, the marvelous bonding, mutual obligation, and reciprocity of kinship is offset by the generally hostile, suspicious, if not down right enmity, toward other tribes and strangers. In the less organized realms of tribal life, strangers and other tribes pose real and serious threats to the freedom, welfare, and sanctity of the people. Competition for productive territory is inevitable and deadly. Blood must be shed to win good ground. Blood must be shed to defend good ground. Failure dooms the people to poverty, misery, and extinction.

But for the most part, the enemy was concentrated by geography. You knew who they were and where they were. All those of a common tribe were living together in the same land. The same could be said about the people. Even when broken into various bands much of the time, you knew who they were, and where they were, more or less all those around you.

The modern "civilized" world has changed the locus of kinship and the enemy. Interspersion rules. There are always some to whom we feel the bonds and obligations of kinship, but they are now often widely dispersed geographically. The same is true for the enemy. The enemy now comes at us most often as individuals. Those that would harm the people without conscience are also dispersed, seemingly at random throughout the echelons and ranges of "civilized" society.

The key is to observe and study how other men treat other people, especially children, pets, and the elderly. Even the best facade by the most practiced sociopath eventually gives itself away. Very young children and pets are especially good miscreant detectors.

The Nerd-Jock Stupidity

One of the sorriest twists to modern male culture is the schism created by the nerd and jock stereotypes. The nerd is a physical geek and wimp, but proficient in high technology and other educated pursuits. The jock is physically proficient and able, but ignorant and contemptuous of intellectual achievement. Both these stereotypes are grossly imbalanced, but youth readily class themselves accordingly.

The dog soldier is a balanced human being. He combines and develops brains and brawn, courage and cunning, increasing and bettering his capabilities across the board, free to range over any or all the fields of human endeavor and accomplishment. All prowess, physical and mental, is valued and respected.

To say that any part of human potential and improvement is alright to neglect and leave undeveloped is to believe that God should have made us lesser animals than we are. Would you rather be a chimpanzee? If you think you are either a nerd or a jock, that's how you rate. Everything any human can do is something that all humans can address, explore and develop beyond where they are now. Why else be human?

The Anti-Dog Soldier

We often come to understand a thing best when we study what it is not. Consider those that might be found wanting for reasons other than defects in character, those who fall short for lack of ability or for caricature in personality. You cannot fault the meek for caving into the coercions of a bully. But if they spread calumny on their own accord, you can. You cannot fault the obnoxious for merely being annoying, but if they purposely offend, you can. While sometimes dangerous, and usually unreliable, these souls are not the enemy.

The enemy, instead, are those who fail the virtues of character, persons who disparage and trample upon the rights and dignity of others, devoid of the sense of kinship and the mutual obligations demanded by a culture of freedom. These are the miscreant and the malformed.

If one wants to know and understand all the twists, dry rot, and putrifications of malformed human character, they must study Freud, and he is only of marginal help. What will be offered here are enough evidences to define the ignoble as the real and present antithesis of finer human attainments.

The Names By Which We Know Them

Phonies, blamers, skunks, whiners, complainers, bastards, jerks, assholes, snakes, liars, frauds, cons, wiseguys, prima donnas, hypocrites, pricks, administrators, louts, creeps, villains, cads, scumbags, slimeballs, bloodsuckers, bullies, blowhards, lunatics, ingrates, pissants, rakes, sons of bitches, malingers, shirkers, rats, pigs, dickheads, gutless wonders, halfwits, loons, the inane, and the insane.

Scoundrels, twits, fiends, pimps, hoods, bums, jokes, clowns, rotten eggs, misers, scrooges, egotists, blockheads, thieves, monkeys, polecats, lizards, buttheads, bureaucrats, smartasses, cowards, sycophants, suckups, goons, nazis, tyrants, false prophets, knaves, sadists, hatemongers, finks and mad dogs.

The Behaviors Which Prove Them

The anti-kinship behaviors and conduct of the enemy are legion, perhaps infinite. What is offered here are enough instances of circumstantial evidence for you to get the idea.

People who persuade you to follow a certain course of action against your inclination and recommendations as a favor to them, and when later events disappoint or fail, blame you, expect you to make good, and to tolerate their chastisements as due penance.

People accuse you of a personal defect, of being insensitive, sexist, arrogant, but who refuse to supply concrete reasons, acting like you should know, and that not knowing is even a greater defect.

People who talk only about themselves, forcing and reforcing your attention on them, and if you do not indulge, put you down in rude, unkind terms.

People who are unfair, like it, relish doing you in, expecting fully to have their way again.

People who believe that their way of living is better, more right, and point to their pile of material possessions as compared to yours to prove it.

People who make a mistake, lie to cover it, spinning more lies to keep the lie alive, expecting you to buy them all without critical thought, when a simple, acceptable admission of error would spare all the hassle and contrivance.

People who through carelessness, recklessness, or sheer incompetence create needless situations where good and innocent people get drug in, drug down, hurt or killed, while they escape unharmed.

People who think of themselves, first, second, third, fourth,....

People who drive bumper to bumper at 70 miles per hour by the dozens, or side by side for miles at 60.

People who say they will do a thing, but only to sound good. If you actually rely upon them, you end up sunk.

People who turn dangerously in front of you, buried in their cell phone, and when you swerve dramatically to avoid collision, shoot you a dirty look and gesture, as if it were your fault to dare be on their road.

People who fan their anger in response to an honest mistake, ignoring your professions of well meaningness, in order to abuse you.

People who take credit for what you do, putting you down and closing you out in the process.

People who fix things that ain't broke.

People who are rude.

People who spread calumny, lies and mistruths about you behind your back, running you down in front of others, out of meanness, spite, or envy, all the while being nice to your face.

People who betray without compunction.

People who use the power of their position to deliver harm and hurt when you are defenseless, out of petty jealousy and malefic spite.

People who look down their noses at you.

People who kick you and twist the knife when you are down and out.

People who prejudge you, badly and wrongly, closing their minds tight like a vise to evidences to the contrary.

People who show contempt.

People who disdain lending aid and assistance when you are needy and without recourse.

People who say they will stand by and behind you to the end of something, but who wimp out, bogey, and run like hell when the going gets tough, leaving you out in the cold to fend for yourself.

People who do lousy work and expect you to like it and not complain.

People who nurse petty grudges until such time as to when they can get more than even.

People who pick upon the weaker of the kinship, abusing them without consideration in foul speech and rude manner.

People who envy what you do and criticize you for it; who covet what you have and disparage it to others.

People who believe your misfortune or bad luck are due to character defects in you that they can find no sign of in themselves.

People who are dangerous, not because of presence or prowess, but because they are physically, or emotionally, or mentally, out of control.

People who are ready and willing to cast the first stone, certain they are free of sanction, blame, or sin.

People who do unto others before others can do unto them.

People who decry the mote in another's eye when they have a tree growing in theirs.

People who blame others for their plights and so excuse themselves from any responsibility.

People who cheat without conscience, and then bluff and bully others when caught.

People who have emotional problems and take it out on you, innocent bystanders, children and dogs.

People who say they want to help, but really just want to spy on your life out of prurient interest.

People who take your kindnesses and goodwill as something you owe them.

People who go out of their way to annoy you to get your attention on them, or cause you a petty injury in a way they can excuse as accidental.

People who see something as plain as day one way, and declare it another.

People who ask for and take your help and assistance, but who then find fault with it, trying every ploy possible to get out of returning the favor when you need some providence.

People who ignore, or refuse to see, the truth, because they didn't think of it first, or because someone they look down upon speaks it.

People who obsessively compare your thoughts, beliefs and manners according to their conformity to theirs to your disadvantage, seeking and securing reason to place themselves above you.

In general, anybody who mistreats people and acts only for themselves, folks you cannot count on when riding and crossing the rivers of real human living.

IN THE WORDS OF OTHERS

Real, Fancied, and Imagined

Stealth, Surprise, Shock.

George Rogers Clark

The country demands bold, persistent experimentation. It is common sense to take a method and try it; if it fails, admit it frankly and try another. But above all, try something.

Franklin Roosevelt

It's a complex fate, being American, and one of the responsibilities it entails is fighting against a superstitious valuation of Europe.

Henry James

Do the sane thing.

William Darby

No one can make you feel inferior without your consent.

Eleanor Roosevelt

I wish to be useful, and every kind of service, necessary to the public good, becomes honorable by being necessary.

Nathan Hale

The force of character is cumulative.
Emerson

When doing the first things first, make sure they are the right things.
Raven Walker

Up, Sluggard, and waste not life; in the grave will be sleeping enough.
Benjamin Franklin

Aim above morality. Be not simply good; be good for something.
Thoreau

You can only protect your liberties in this world by protecting the other man's freedom. You can only be free if I am free.
Clarence Darrow

They that can give up essential liberty to purchase a little temporary safety, deserve neither liberty nor safety.
Benjamin Franklin

If a man hasn't discovered something that he will die for, he isn't fit to live.
Martin Luther King

Live so that you can look any man in the eye and tell him to go to hell.
Unknown

Grief can take care of itself, but to get the full value of joy you must have somebody to divide it with.

Mark Twain

When walking the plank, get a good running start.

Raven Walker

We become not a melting pot but a beautiful mosaic. Different people, different beliefs, different yearnings, different hopes, different dreams.

Jimmy Carter

They proclaimed to all the world the revolutionary doctrine of the divine rights of the common man. That doctrine has ever since been the heart of the American faith.

Dwight Eisenhower

We fight, get beat, rise, and fight again.

Nathanael Greene

We fight not to enslave, but to set a country free, and to make room upon the earth for honest men to live in.

Thomas Paine

People who cannot recognize a palpable absurdity are very much in the way of civilization.

Agnes Repplier

Freedom has its life in the hearts, the actions, and the spirit of men and so it must be daily earned and refreshed—else like a flower cut from its life giving roots, it will wither and die.

Dwight Eisenhower

Do the hardest part first.

Raven Walker

We cannot chose freedom established on a hierarchy of degrees of freedom, on a caste system of equality like military rank. We must be free not beause we claim freedom, but because we practice it.

William Faulkner

I never did anything worth doing by accident, nor did any of my inventions come by accident; they came by work.

Thomas Edison

The truth has always been dangerous to the rule of the rogue, the exploiter, the robber. So the truth must be ruthlessly suppressed.

Eugene Debs

No people ever lost their liberties unless they themselves first became corrupt. The people are the safeguards of their own liberties, and I rely wholly on them to guard themselves.

Andrew Jackson

God grants liberty only to those who love it, and are always ready to guard and defend it.

Daniel Webster

As long as the world shall last there will be wrongs, and if no man objected and no man rebelled, those wrongs would last forever.
Clarence Darrow

Nothing astonishes men so much as common sense and plain dealing.
Emerson

Liberty, when it begins to take root, is a plant of rapid growth.
George Washington

Measure a man from the neck up.
Al Maguire

Injustice anywhere is a threat to justice everywhere.
Martin Luther King

The best way out of a difficulty is through it.
Unknown

It is part of the American character to consider nothing as desperate, to surmount every difficulty by resolution and contrivance.
Thomas Jefferson

Military power will never awe a sensible American tamely to surrender his liberty.
Samuel Adams

Let us therefore animate and encourage each other, and show the whole world that a Freeman, contending for liberty on his own ground, is superior to any slavish mercenary on earth.

George Washington

I would define true courage to be perfect sensibility of the measure of danger, and a mental willingness to endure it.

William Tecumseh Sherman

Of more worth is one honest man to society, and in the sight of God, than all the crowned ruffians that ever lived.

Thomas Paine

I expect to pass through this world but once; any good thing, therefore, that I can do, or any kindness that I can show to any fellow creature, let me do it now; let me not defer or neglect it, for I shall not pass this way again.

Unknown

Beware of all enterprises that require new clothes.

Thoreau

The greatest accomplishment is not in never falling, but in rising again after you fall.

Vince Lombardi

Push the envelope.

Chuck Yeager

Don't forget nothing.
> Robert Rogers

Men do not follow titles. They follow courage.
> William Wallace

He who conquers himself is strong.
> Tao te Chin

If a man does not keep pace with his companions, perhaps it is beause he hears a different drummer. Let him step to the music which he hears, however measured or far away.
> Thoreau

Liberty is the only thing you cannot have unless you are willing to give it to others.
> William Allen White

Far and away the best prize that life offers is the chance to work hard at work worth doing.
> Theodore Roosevelt

There is no limit to the good you can do if you don't care who gets the credit.
> George Marshall

The wisest man preaches no doctrines; he has no scheme; he sees no rafter, not even a cobweb, against the heavens. It is clear sky.
> Thoreau

We are not afraid to follow truth wherever it may lead, nor to tolerate any error so long as reason is left free to combat it.
                                                      Thomas Jefferson

Shallow men believe in luck, believe in circumstances. Strong men believe in cause and effect.
                                                      Emerson

The universe is so vast and ageless that the life of one man can only be measured by the size of his sacrifice.
                                                      Flying Officer VA Rosewarne, RAF

It is better to live one day as a lion than a hundred years as a sheep.
                                                      Italian proverb

People sleep peaceably in their beds at night only because rough men stand ready to do violence on their behalf.
                                                      George Orwell

Where liberty dwells, there is my country.
                                                      Benjamin Franklin

The truth is, all might be free if they valued freedom, and defended it as they ought.
                                                      Samuel Adams

Decency—generousity—cooperation—assistance in trouble—devotion to duty; these are the things that are of greater value than surface appearances and customs.

Dwight Eisenhower

There is no end to the sufficiency of character. It can afford to wait; it can do without what is called success.

Emerson

The difficult we do immediately. The impossible takes a little longer.

U.S. Army Forces in WWII

Only two things are infinite, the universe and human stupidty, and I'm not sure about the former.

Albert Einstein

Everything I did in my life that was worthwhile I caught hell for.

Earl Warren

Many men die at twenty-five and aren't buried until they are seventy-five.

Benjamin Franklin

It is veneer, rouge, aestheticism, art museums, new theaters, etc. that make America impotent. The good things are football, kindness, and jazz bands.

Santayana

We must combine the toughness of the serpent and the softness of the dove, a tough mind and a tender heart.

Martin Luther King

I leave this rule for others when I'm dead. Be always sure you're right—
then go ahead.

Davy Crockett

There ain't no rules around here! We're trying to accomplish something!
Thomas Edison

When a man is finally boxed and he has no choice, he begins to decorate his box.

John Steinbeck

Trust men, and they will be true to you; treat them greatly, and they
will show themselves great.

Emerson

All the armies of Europe, Asia, and Africa combined, with all the treasure of the earth in their military chest, with a Bonaparte for a commander,
could not, by force, take a drink from the Ohio, or make a track on the
Blue Ridge, in a trail of a thousand years.

Abraham Lincoln

We are the pioneers of the world; the advance guard sent on through
the wilderness of untried things to break a new path in the New World
that is ours. In our youth is our strength; in our inexperience, our wisdom.

Herman Melville

Some men appear to feel that they belong to a pariah caste. They fear to
offend, they bend and apologize, and walk through life with a timid step.

Emerson

Every action in company, ought to be with some sign of respect to those present.

George Washington

Generousity is the flower of justice.

Nathaniel Hawthorne

Where sense in wanting, everything is wanting.

Benjamin Franklin

Attack another's rights and you destroy your own.

John Jay Chapman

Equality in society beats inequality, whether the latter be of the British-aristocratic sort or of the domestic-slavery sort.

Abraham Lincoln

Wise men talk because they have something to say; fools talk beause they have to say something.

Plato

I know of no more encouraging fact than the unquestionable ability of man to elevate his life by conscious endeavor.

Thoreau

Always do right—this will gratify some and astonish the rest.

Mark Twain

Use no hurtful deceit; think innocently and justly and, if you speak, speak accordingly.

> Benjamin Franklin

Sometimes you have to walk on water just to keep from drowning.

> Raven Walker

God Did not Make a Man of my Prinsipal to be Lost.

> Daniel Boone

www.ingramcontent.com/pod-product-compliance
Lightning Source LLC
Chambersburg PA
CBHW021600280526
45784CB00001BA/431